1 MONTH OF FREE READING

at

www.ForgottenBooks.com

By purchasing this book you are eligible for one month membership to ForgottenBooks.com, giving you unlimited access to our entire collection of over 1,000,000 titles via our web site and mobile apps.

To claim your free month visit:
www.forgottenbooks.com/free193910

* Offer is valid for 45 days from date of purchase. Terms and conditions apply.

ISBN 978-0-483-66467-8
PIBN 10193910

This book is a reproduction of an important historical work. Forgotten Books uses state-of-the-art technology to digitally reconstruct the work, preserving the original format whilst repairing imperfections present in the aged copy. In rare cases, an imperfection in the original, such as a blemish or missing page, may be replicated in our edition. We do, however, repair the vast majority of imperfections successfully; any imperfections that remain are intentionally left to preserve the state of such historical works.

Forgotten Books is a registered trademark of FB &c Ltd.
Copyright © 2018 FB &c Ltd.
FB &c Ltd, Dalton House, 60 Windsor Avenue, London, SW19 2RR.
Company number 08720141. Registered in England and Wales.

For support please visit www.forgottenbooks.com

THE
HERO OF THE HUMBER;

OR, THE

HISTORY OF THE LATE

MR. JOHN ELLERTHORPE

(FOREMAN OF THE HUMBER DOCK GATES, HULL),

BEING A RECORD OF

REMARKABLE INCIDENTS IN HIS CAREER AS A SAILOR; HIS CONVERSION AND CHRISTIAN USEFULNESS; HIS UNEQUALLED SKILL AS A SWIMMER, AND HIS EXPLOITS ON THE WATER, WITH A MINUTE ACCOUNT OF HIS DEEDS OF DARING IN SAVING, WITH HIS OWN HANDS, ON SEPARATE AND DISTINCT OCCASIONS, UPWARDS OF FORTY PERSONS FROM DEATH BY DROWNING: TOGETHER WITH AN ACCOUNT OF HIS LAST AFFLICTION, DEATH, ETC.

BY THE

REV. HENRY WOODCOCK,

AUTHOR OF 'POPERY UNMASKED,' 'WONDERS OF GRACE,' ETC.

'My tale is simple and of humble birth,
A tribute of respect to real worth.'

SECOND EDITION.

LONDON:
S. W. Partridge, 9, Paternoster Row; Wesleyan Book Room, 66, Paternoster Row; Primitive Methodist Book Room, 6, Sutton Street, Commercial Road, E.; and of all Booksellers.
1880.

ALFORD:
J. HORNER, PRINTER,
MARKET-PLACE.

TO
THE SEAMEN OF GREAT BRITAIN,

TO WHOSE

SKILL, COURAGE, AND ENDURANCE,

ENGLAND OWES MUCH OF HER GREATNESS,

THIS VOLUME—

CONTAINING A RECORD OF THE CHARACTER AND DEEDS OF ONE,

WHO, FOR UPWARDS OF THIRTY YEARS,

BRAVED THE HARDSHIPS AND PERILS OF A SAILOR'S LIFE,

AND

WHOSE GALLANTRY AND HUMANITY

WON FOR HIM THE TITLE

OF

'THE HERO OF THE HUMBER,'

IS MOST RESPECTFULLY DEDICATED,

WITH THE EARNEST PRAYER

THAT THEY MAY EMBRACE THAT BENIGN RELIGION

WHICH NOT ONLY RESCUED THE 'HERO' FROM THE EVILS IN WHICH

HE HAD SO LONG INDULGED,

AND ENRICHED HIM WITH THE GRACES OF THE

CHRISTIAN CHARACTER,

BUT ALSO GAVE

A BRIGHTER GLOW AND GREATER ENERGY

TO THAT

COURAGE, GALLANTRY, AND HUMANITY

BY WHICH HE HAD BEEN LONG DISTINGUISHED.

THE AUTHOR.

PREFACE

TO THE SECOND EDITION.

Mr. Gladstone, in a recent lecture thus defines a hero: quoting Latham's definition of a hero,—'a man eminent for bravery,' he said he was not satisfied with that, because bravery might be mere animal bravery. Carlyle had described Napoleon I. as a great hero. 'Now he (Mr. Gladstone) was not prepared to admit that Napoleon was a hero. He was certainly one of the most extraordinary men ever born. There was more power concentrated in that brain than in any brain probably born for centuries. That he was a great man in the sense of being a man of transcendent power, there was no doubt; but his life was tainted with selfishness from beginning to end, and he was not ready to admit that a man whose life was fundamentally tainted with selfishness was a hero. A greater hero than Napoleon was the captain of a ship which was run down in the Channel three or four years ago, who, when the ship was quivering, and the water was gurgling round her, and the boats had been lowered to save such persons as could be saved, stood by the bulwark with a pistol in his hand and threatened to shoot dead the first man who endeavoured to get into the boat until every woman and child was provided for. His true idea of a hero was this:—A hero was a man who must have ends beyond himself, in casting himself as it were out of himself, and must pursue these ends by means which were honourable, the lawful means, otherwise he might degenerate into a wild enthusiast. He must do this without distortion or disturbance of his nature as a man, because there were cases of men who were heroes in great part, but who were so excessively given to certain ideas and objects of their own, that they lost all the proportion of their nature. There were other heroes, who, by giving undue prominence to one idea, lost the just proportion of things, and became simply men of one idea. A man to be a hero must pursue ends beyond himself by legitimate means. He must pursue them as a man, not as a dreamer. Not to give to some one idea disproportionate weight which it did not deserve, and forget everything else which belonged to the perfection and excellence of human nature. If he did all this he was a hero, even if he had not very great powers; and if he had great powers, then he was a consummate hero.'

Now, if we cannot claim for the late Mr. Ellerthorpe 'great powers' of intellect, we are quite sure that all who read the following pages will agree that the title bestowed upon him by his grateful and admiring townsman,—'THE HERO OF THE HUMBER,' was well and richly deserved. He was a 'Hero,' though he lived in a humble cottage. He was a man of heroic sacrifices; his services were of the noblest kind; he sought the highest welfare of his fellow-creatures with an energy never surpassed; his generous and impulsive nature found its highest happiness in promoting the welfare of others. He is held as a benefactor in the fond recollection of thousands of his fellow countrymen, and he received rewards far more valuable and satisfying than those which his Queen and Government bestowed upon him: more lasting than the gorgeous pageantries and emblazoned escutcheon that reward the hero of a hundred battles.

>The warrior's deeds may win
> An earthly fame, but deeds by mercy wrought,
>Are heaven's own register within:
> Not one shall be forgot.

The scene of most of his gallant exploits in rescuing human lives was 'The river Humber;' hence the title given him by a large gathering of his fellow townsmen.

The noble river Humber, upon which the town of Kingston-upon-Hull is seated, may be considered the Thames of the Midland and Northern Counties of England. It divides the East Riding of Yorkshire from Lincolnshire, during the whole of its course, and is formed by the junction of the Ouse and the Trent. At Bromfleet, it receives the little river Foulness, and rolling its vast collection of waters eastward, in a stream enlarged to between two and three miles in breadth, washes the town of Hull, where it receives the river of the same name. Opposite to Hedon and Paul, which are a few miles below Hull, the Humber widens into a vast estuary, six or seven miles in breadth, and then directs it course past Great Grimsby to the German Ocean, which it enters at Spurn Head. No other river system collects waters from so many important towns as this famous stream. 'The Humber,' says a recent writer, 'resembling the trunk of a vast tree spreading its branches in every direction, commands, by the numerous rivers which it receives, the navigation and trade of a very extensive and commercial part of England.'

The Humber, between its banks, occupies an area of about one hundred and twenty-five square miles. The rivers Ouse and Trent which, united, form the Humber, receive the waters of the Aire, Calder, Don, Old Don, Derwent, Idle, Sheaf, Soar, Nidd, Yore, Wharfe, &c., &c.

From the waters of this far-famed river—the Humber—Mr. Ellerthorpe rescued thirty-one human beings from drowning.

For the rapid sale of 3,500 copies of the 'Life of the Hero,' the Author thanks a generous public. A series of articles extracted from the first edition appeared in '*Home Words.*' An illustrated article also appears in Cassell's '*Heroes of Britain in Peace and War,*' in which the writer speaks of the present biography as '*That very interesting book in which the history of Ellerthorpe's life is told.* (P. 1. 2. PART XI.) The Author trusts that the present edition, containing an account of 'The Hero's' last affliction, death, funeral, etc., will render the work additionally interesting.

THE WRITER.

53, *Leonard Street, Hull, Aug. 4th,* 1880.

CONTENTS.

CHAP.		PAGE
I.	His wicked and reckless career	1
II.	His conversion and inner experience	6
III.	His Christian labours	14
IV.	His staunch teetotalism	22
V.	His bold adventures on the water	31
VI.	His method of rescuing the drowning	44
VII.	His gallant and humane conduct in rescuing the drowning	51
VIII.	The honoured hero	95
IX.	His general character, death, etc.	116
X.	The hero's funeral	122

The Hero of the Humber.

CHAPTER I.

HIS WICKED AND RECKLESS CAREER AS A SAILOR.

'THE fine old town of Hull has many institutions of which it is deservedly proud. There is the Charter house, a monument of practical piety of the days of old. There is the Literary and Philosophical Institute, with its large and valuable library, and its fine museum, each of which is most handsomely housed. There is the new Town Hall, the work of one of the town's most gifted sons. There is the tall column erected in honour of WILBERFORCE, in the days when the representatives of the law were expected to obey the laws, and when the cultivation of a philanthropic feeling towards the negro had not gone out of fashion. There is the Trinity House, with its magnificent endowments, which have for more than five centuries blessed the mariners of the port, and which is now represented by alms-houses, so numerous, so large, so externally beautiful, and so trimly kept as to be both morally and architecturally among the noblest ornaments of the town. There is the Port of Hull Society, with its chapel, its reading-rooms, its orphanage, its seaman's mission, all most generously supported. There is that leaven of ancient pride which also may be classed among the institutions of the place, and which operates in giving to a population by no means wealthy a habit of respectability, and a look for the most part well-to-do. But among none of these will be found the institution to which we are about to refer. The institution that we are to-day concerned to honour is compact, is self-supporting, is eminently philanthropic, has done more good with very limited means than any other, and is so much an object of legitimate pride, that we have pleasure in making this unique institution more generally known. A life-saving institution that has in the course of a few brief years rescued about fifty people from drowning, and that has done so without expectation of reward, deserves to be named, and the name of this institution is simply that of a comparatively poor man—JOHN ELLERTHORPE, dock gate-keeper, at the entrance of the Humber Dock.'

Such was the strain in which the *Sheffield Daily Telegraph*, in a Leader (March 17th, 1868), spoke of the character and doings of him whom a grateful and admiring town entitled 'THE HERO OF THE HUMBER.'

He was born at Rawcliffe, a small village near Snaith, Yorkshire, in the year 1806. His ancestors, as far as we can trace them, were all connected with the sea-faring life. His father, John Ellerthorpe, owned a 'Keel' which sailed between Rawcliffe and the large towns in the West Riding of Yorkshire, and John often accompanied him during his voyages. His mother was a woman of great practical sagacity and unquestionable honesty and piety, and from her young John extended many of the high and noble qualities which distinguished his career. Much of his childhood, however, was passed at the 'Anchor' public house, Rawcliffe, kept by his paternal grandmother, where he early became an adept swearer and a lover of the pot, and for upwards of forty years—to use his own language—he was 'a drunken blackard.'

When John was ten years of age his father removed to Hessle. About this time John heard that flaming evangelist, the Rev. William Clowes, preach near the 'old pump' at Hessle, and he retired from the service with good resolutions in his breast, and sought a place of prayer. Soon after he heard the famous John Oxtoby preach, and he says, 'I was truly converted under his sermon, and for sometime I enjoyed a clear sense of forgiveness.' His mother's heart rejoiced at the change; but from his father, who was an habitual drunkard, he met with much opposition and persecution, and being but a boy, and possessing a very impressionable nature, John soon joined his former corrupt associates and cast off, for upwards of thirty years, even the form of prayer.

Ellerthorpe was born with a passion for salt water. He was reared on the banks of a well navigated river, the Humber, and, in his boyhood, he liked not only to be on the water, but *in* it. He also accompanied his father on his voyages, and when left at home he spent most of his time in the company of seamen, and these awakened within him the tastes and ambition of a sailor. He went to sea when fourteen years of age, and for three years sailed in the brig 'Jubilee,' then trading between Hull and London. The next four years were spent under Captain Knill, on board of the 'Westmoreland,' trading between Hull and Quebec, America. Afterwards he spent several years in the Baltic trade. When the steam packet, 'Magna Charter,' began to run between Hull and New Holland, John became a sailor on board and afterwards Captain of the vessel. He next became Captain of a steamer that ran between Barton and Hessle. He then sailed in a vessel between Hull and America. In 1845, he entered the service of the Hull Dock Company, in which situation he remained up to the time of his death.

Fifty years ago our sailors, generally speaking, were a grossly wicked class of men. A kind of special license to indulge in all kinds of sin was given to the rough and hardy men whose occupation was on the mighty deep. Landsmen, while comfortably seated round a winter's fire, listening to the storm and tempest raging without, were not only struck with amazement at the courage and endurance of sailors in exposing themselves to the elements, but, influenced by their imagination, magnified the energy and bravery that overcame them. Peasants gazed with wild astonishment on the village lad returned, after a few years absence, a veritable 'Jack tar.' The credulity of these delighted listeners tempted Jack to 'spin his yarns,' and tell his tales of nautical adventures, real or imaginary. Hence, he was everywhere greeted with a genial and profuse hospitality. The best seat in the house, the choicest drinks in the cellar, were for Jack. Our ships of commerce, like so many shuttles, were rapidly weaving together the nations of the earth in friendly amity. Besides, a romantic sentiment and feeling, generated to a great extent by the victories which our invincible navy had won during the battles of the Nile, and perpetuated by Nelson's sublime battle cry, 'England expects every man to do his duty,' helped to swell the tide of sympathy in favour of the sailor. Under these circumstances Jack became Society's indulged and favoured guest; and yet he remained outside of it. 'Peculiarities incident to his profession, and which ought to have been corrected by education and religion, became essential features of character in the public mind. A sailor became an idea—a valuable menial in the service of the commonwealth, but as strange and as eccentric in his habits as the walk of some amphibious animal, or web-footed aquatic on land. To purchase a score of watches, and to fry them in a pan with beer, to charter half a dozen coaches, and invite foot passengers inside, while he 'kept on deck,' or in any way to scatter his hard earnings of a twelvemonth in as many hours, was considered frolicsome thoughtlessness, which was more than compensated by the throwing away of a purse of gold to some poor woman in distress.' Landsharks and crimps beset the young sailor in every sea port; low music halls and dingy taverns and beer shops presented their attractions; and there the 'jolly tars' used to swallow their poisonous compounds, and roar out ribald songs, and dance their clumsy fandangoes with the vilest outcasts of society. 'It is a necessary evil,' said some; 'it is the very nature of sailors, poor fellows.' While the thoughtless multitude were immensely tickled with Jack's mad antics and drolleries. Generous to a fault to all who were in need, Jack's motto was:—

While there's a shot in the locker, a messmate to bless,
It shall always be shared with a friend in distress.

Amid such scenes as these our friend spent a great portion of his youth and early manhood. The loud ribald laugh, the vile jest and song, the midnight uproar, the drunken row, the flaunting dress and impudent gestures of the wretched women who frequent our places of ungodly resort—amid such scenes as these, did he waste his precious time and squander away much of his hard earned money. But though a wild and reckless sailor, his warm and generous heart was ever impelling him to noble and generous deeds. If he sometimes became the dupe of the designing, and indulged in the wild revelry of passion, at other times he gave way to an outburst of generosity bordering on prodigality, relieving the necessities of the poor, or true to the instincts of a British tar standing up to redress the wrongs of the oppressed.

CHAPTER II.

HIS CONVERSION AND INNER EXPERIENCE.

WHEN far away on the sea, and while mingling in all the dissipated scenes of a sailor's life, John would sometimes think of those youthful days—the only sunny spot in his life's journey—when he 'walked in the fear of the Lord and in the comfort of the Holy Ghost.' Serious thoughts would rise in his mind, and those seeds of truth, sown in his heart while listening to Clowes and Oxtoby, and which for years seemed dead, would be quickened into life. He had often wished to hear Mr. Clowes once more, and on seeing a placard announcing that he would preach at the opening of the Nile Street Chapel, Hull (1846), he hastened home, and, sailor-like, quaintly observed to his wife, 'Why that old Clowes is living and is going to preach. Let's go and hear him.' On the following Sunday he went to the chapel, but it was so many years since he had been to God's house that he now felt ashamed to enter, and for some minutes he wandered to and fro in front of the chapel. At length he ventured to go in, and sat down in a small pew just within the door. His mind was deeply affected, and ere the next Sabbath he had taken two sittings in the chapel.

About this time, the Rev. Charles Jones, of blessed memory, began his career as a missionary in Hull. He laboured during six years, with great success, in the streets, and yards, and alleys of the town; and scores now in heaven and hundreds on their way thither, will, through all eternity, have to bless God that Primitive Methodism ever sent him to labour in Hull. The Rev. G. Lamb prepared the people to receive him by styling him 'a bundle of love.' John went to hear him, and charmed by his preaching and allured by the grace of God, his religious feelings were deepened. Soon after this, and through the labours of Mr. Lamb, he obtained peace with God, and I have heard him say at our lovefeasts, 'Jones knocked me down, but it was Mr. Lamb that picked me up.'

Being invited by two Christian friends to attend a class meeting on the following Sabbath morning, he went. As he sat in that old room in West Street Chapel, a thousand gloomy thoughts and fearful apprehensions crossed his mind, and casting many a glance towards the door, he '*felt as though he must dart out.*' But when Mr. John Sissons, the leader of the class, said, with his usual kind smile and sympathizing look:—'I'm glad to see you,' and then proceeded to give him suitable council and encouragement, John's heart melted and his eyes filled with tears; and, on being invited to repeat his visit on the following Sabbath, he at once consented. One of the friends who had accompanied him to the class, said, 'Now God has sown the seed of grace in your heart and the enemy will try to sow tares, but if you resist the devil he will flee from you,' and scarcely had John left the room *ere the battle began.* 'Oh, what a fool' he thought, 'I was to promise to go again,' and when he got home he said to his wife, 'I've been to class, and what is worse, I have promised to go again, and I dar'nt run off.' Mrs. Ellerthorpe, who had begun to watch with some interest her husband's struggles, wisely replied, 'Go, for you cannot go to a better place, I intend to go to Mr. Jones' class.' All the next week John was in great perplexity, thinking, 'What can I say if I go? If I tell them the same tale I told them last week they will say I've got it off by memory.' On the following Sabbath morning he was in the street half resolved not to go to class, when he thought, 'Did'nt my friend say the devil would tempt me and that I was to resist him? Perhaps it is the devil that is filling me with these distressing feelings, but I'll resist him,' and, suiting his action to his words, in a moment, John was seen darting along the street at his utmost speed; nor did he pause till, panting and almost breathless, he found himself seated in the vestry of the Primitive Methodist Chapel, West Street. He regarded that meeting as the turning point in his spiritual history, and in the review it possessed to him an undying charm. There a full, free, and present salvation was pressed on the people. The short way to the cross was pointed out. The blessedness of the man whose transgression is forgiven was realized. The direct and comforting witness of the Holy Spirit to the believer's adoption was proclaimed. And there believers were exhorted to grow richer in holiness and riper in knowledge every day. And while John sat and listened to God's people, he felt a divine power coming down from on high, which he could not comprehend, but which, however, he joyously experienced. He joined the class that morning and continued a member five years, when he became connected with our new chapel in Thornton Street. Around these services in the old vestry at West Street, cluster the grateful recollections of many now living and of numbers who have crossed the flood. How often has that room resounded with the cries of penitent sinners and the songs of rejoicing believers?

Soon after our friend had united himself with the people of God he paid a visit to his mother, who was in a dying state. It was on a beautiful Sabbath morning, in the month of June, and while walking along the road, between Hull and Hessle, and reflecting on the change he had experienced, he was filled 'unutterably full of glory and of God.' That morning, with its glorious visitation of grace, he never forgot. His soul had new feelings; his heart throbbed with a new, a strange, a divine joy. Peace reigned within and all around was lovely. The sun seemed to shine more brightly, and the birds sang a sweeter song. The flowers wore a more beautiful aspect, and the very grass seemed clothed in a more vivid green. It was like a little heaven below. 'As I walked along,' he says, 'I shouted, glory, glory, glory, and I am sure if a number of sinners had heard me they would have thought me mad.'

But was he mad? Did not the pentecostal converts 'eat their meat with gladness and singleness of heart, praising God?' Did not the converts in Samaria 'make great joy in the city?' Did not the Ethiopian Eunuch, having obtained salvation, *go on his way rejoicing?*' And Charles Wesley, four days after his conversion, thus expressed the joy he felt—

> I rode on the sky so happy was I,
> Nor envied Elijah his seat;
> My soul mounted higher in a chariot of fire
> As the moon was under my feet.

And surely God's people have as much right to give utterance to their joy as the dupes of the devil have to give expression to theirs; and though the religion of the Saviour requires us to surrender many pleasures, and endure peculiar sorrows, yet it is, supremely, the religion of peace, joy, and overflowing gladness.

Mr. Ellerthorpe was never guilty of proclaiming with the trumpet tongue of a Pharisee, either what he felt or did, and though he kept a carefully written diary, extending over several volumes, and the reading of which has been a great spiritual treat to the writer of this book,—revealing, as it does, the secret of that intense earnestness, unbending integrity, active benevolence, and readiness for every good word and work by which our friend's religious career was distinguished,—yet of that diary our space will permit us to make but the briefest use. Take the following extracts:—

'January 1, 1852.—I, John Ellerthorpe, here in the presence of my God, before whom I bow, covenant to live nearer to Him than I have done in the year that has rolled into eternity.'

RESOLUTIONS.

'1st. I will bow three times a day in secret.

2nd. I will attend all the means of grace I can.

3rd. I will visit what sick I can.

4th. I will speak ill of no man.

5th. I will hear nothing against any man, especially those who belong to the same society.

6th. I will respect all men, especially Christians.

7th. I will pray for a revival.

8th. I will guard against all bad language and ill feeling.

9th. I will never speak rash to any man.

10th. I will be honest in all my dealings.

11th. I will always speak the truth.

12th. I will never contract a debt without a proper prospect of payment.

13th. I will read three chapters of the Bible daily.

14th. I will get all to class I possibly can.

15th. I will set a good example before all men, and especially my own family.

16th. I will not be bound for any man.

17th. I will not argue on scripture with any man.

18th. I will endeavour to improve my time.

19th. I will endeavour to be ready every moment.

20th. I will leave all my concerns in the hands of my God, for Christ's sake. All these I intend, by the help of my God, diligently to perform.'

That he always carried out these resolutions is more than his diary will warrant us to say. He sometimes missed the mark, and came short of his aim. He suffered from a certain hastiness of temper, and ruggedness of disposition, which, to use his own words, 'cost him a vast deal of watching and praying. But the Lord,' he adds, 'has helped me in a wonderful manner, and I believe I shall reap if I faint not.' The following extracts from his diary will give some idea of his inner experience :—

'*January* 1850. *5th.*—I feel the hardness of my heart and the littleness of my love, yet I am in a great degree able to deny myself to take up my cross to follow Christ through good and evil report. *7th.*—I feel that I am growing in grace and that I have more power over temptation, and over myself than I had some time since, but I want the witness of full sanctification. *8th.*—What is now the state of my mind? Do I now enjoy an interest in Christ? Am I a child of God? It is suggested by Satan that I am guilty of many imperfections. I know it, but I know also if any man sin, etc. *Feb.* 18*th.*—I feel my heart is very hard and stubborn, that I am proud and haughty and very bad tempered, but God can, and I believe he will, break my rocky heart in pieces. *March 3rd.*—This has been a good Sabbath; we had a good prayer meeting at 7 o'clock, a profitable class at 9, in the school the Lord was with us, and the preaching services were good. *4th.*—Last night I had a severe attack of my old complaint and suffered greatly for many hours, but I called upon God and he delivered me. *16th.*—I am in good health, for which, and the use of my reason, and all the blessings that God bestows upon me, I am thankful. I am unworthy of the least of them. O that I could love God ten thousand times more than I do; for I feel ashamed of myself that I love him so little. *19th.*—I am ill in body but well in soul. The flesh may give way, and the devil may tempt me, and all hell may rage, yet I believe the Lord will bring me through. *April 6th.*—To-day, in the haste of my temper, I called a man a liar. I now feel that I did wrong in the sight of God and man. I am deeply sorry. May God forgive me, and may I sin no more. *May 6th.*— O God make me faithful and give to thy servant the spirit of prayer. Like David, I want to resolve, "Speak, Lord; for thy servant heareth"; like Mary I want to "ponder these things in my heart"; like the Bereans I want to "search the scriptures" daily and in the spirit of Samuel to say "Speak, Lord: for thy servant heareth." *May 20th.*—I am at Hessle feast, and thank God it has been a feast to my soul. I have attended one prayer meeting, two class meetings, three preaching services. Bless God for these means of grace. My little book is full and I do trust I am a better man than when I began to write my diary. *29th.*—My dear wife is very ill, but the Lord does all things well. I know that He can, and believe that He will, raise her up again and that the affliction of her body will turn to the salvation of her soul. *30th.*—I am now laid under fresh obligations to God. He has given me another son. May he be a goodly child, like Moses, and grow up to be a man after God's own heart. *July 3rd.*—This day the Victoria docks have been opened. It has been a day of trial and conflict, for I ran the Packet into a Schooner and did £10 damage. It was a trial of my faith, and through the assistance of God I overcame. *August 20th.*—SUNDAY.—How thankful I am that God has set one day in seven when we can get away from the wear and tear of life and worship Him under our own vine and fig tree none daring to make us afraid. It is all of God's wisdom, and mercy, and goodness. *September 11th.*—To-night I put my wife's name in the class book; may she be a very good member, such a one as Thou wilt own when Thou numbers up Thy jewels. *October 11th.*—I did wrong last night, being quite in a passson at my wife, which grieved her. Lord help me and make me never differ with her again. *12th.*—I feel much better in my soul this morning and will, from this day promise in the strength of grace, never to allow myself to be thrown into a passion again: it grieves my soul, it hurts my mind. 1851. *January 7th.*—Five years this day I entered my present situation under the Hull Dock Company. Then I was a drunken man, and a great swearer; but I thank God he has changed my heart. 18th.—This has been a very troublesome day to my soul. I have been busy with the sunken packet all day and hav'nt had time to get to prayer. My soul feels hungry. 29th.—This has been a day of prayerful anxiety about my son; he has passed his third examination, God having heard my prayer on his behalf. *Feb.* 24th.—I have been to the teetotal meeting and have taken the pledge, and I intend, through the grace of God, to keep as long as I live. *March* 1st.—The Rev. W. Clowes is still alive. May the Lord grant that he may not have much pain. While brother Newton and I were in the room with him we felt it good; O the beauty of seeing a good man in a dying state. May I live the life of the righteous and may my last end be like Mr. Clowes's. 2nd.—The first thing I did this morning was to go and inquire after Mr. Clowes. I found that life was gone and that his happy spirit had taken its flight to heaven. 4th.—I am more than ever convinced of the great advantage we derive from entire sanctification; it preserves the soul in rest amid the toils of life; it gives satisfaction with every situation in which God pleases to place us.'

Sailor like Mr. Ellerthorpe was earnest, impulsive, enthusiastic, carrying a warm ardour and a brisk life into all his duties. He did not love a continual calm, rather he preferred the storm. He did not believe that because he was on board a good ship, had shaped his course aright, and had a compass never losing its polarity, that he would reach port whether he made sail or not, whether he minded his helm or not. He knew he couldn't *drift* into port. With waterlogged and becalmed Christians or those who heaved to crafts expecting to drift to the celestial heaven, he had but little fellowship. Such he would cause to shake out reefs and have yards well trimmed to catch every breeze from the millenial trade winds.

CHAPTER III.

HIS CHRISTIAN LABOURS.

HAVING become a subject of saving grace, Mr. Ellerthorpe felt an earest desire that others should participate in the same benefit. Nor was there any object so dear to his heart, and upon which he was at all times so ready to speak, as the conversion of sinners. He knew he did not possess the requisite ability for preaching the gospel, and therefore he sought out a humbler sphere in which his new-born zeal might spend its fires, and in that sphere he laboured, with remarkable success, during a quarter of a century. I NOW REFER TO THE SICK CHAMBER.

During all that time he took a deep interest in the sick and the dying; and for several years after his conversion, having much time at his disposal, he would often visit as many as twenty families per day, for weeks together. When Cholera, that mysterious disease, with its sudden attacks, its racking cramps, its icy cold touch, and its almost resistless progress, swept through the town of Hull, in the year 1849, leaving one thousand eight hundred and sixty,—or one in forty of the entire population,—*dead*, our friend was at any one's call, and never refused a single application; indeed, he was known as a great visitor of the sick and dying, and was often called in extreme cases to visit those from whom others shrank lest they should catch the contagion of the disorder. The scenes of suffering and distress which he witnessed baffled description. On one occasion he entered a room where a whole family were smitten with cholera. The wife lay cold and dead in one corner of the room, a child had just expired in another corner, and the husband and father was dying, amidst excruciating pain, in the middle of the room. John knelt down and spoke words of Christian comfort to the man, who died in a few moments.

For years, he was in the habit of accompanying Mr. Jones, when visiting the miserable garrets, obscure yards, and wretched alleys in Hull, and was considered his 'right hand man,' in helping to hold open-air services. They often went in company to such wretched localities as 'Leadenhall Square,' then the greatest cesspool of vice in the Port, and, well supplied with tracts, visited every house. During the intervals of public worship, on the Sabbath day, when he might have been enjoying himself in the circle of his family, on a clean hearth, before a bright fire, he was pointing perishing sinners to the Lamb of God. When our new and beautiful chapel in Great Thornton Street was discovered to be on fire, at noon, — March, 1856, he was at the bedside of an afflicted woman, Mrs. Wright, speaking to her of her past sins and of a precious Saviour. He had spent some time with her daily for months, but just at this time he became Foreman of the Victoria Dock and could no longer pay his daily visits to the sick, which greatly distressed Mrs. Wright and others; but duty called him elsewhere and he obeyed its voice. He says, 'I durst not make any fresh engagements to visit the sick, and up to the present time (1867) I have rarely been able to visit, except on the Sabbath day, all my time being required at the dock gates. But on the Sabbath I love to get to the bedside of the sick; nothing does me more good; there my soul is often refreshed and my zeal invigorated.'

Those who are most averse to religion in life, generally desire to share its benefits in death. Their religion is very much like the great coats which persons of delicate health wear in this changeable climate, and which they use in foul weather, but lay aside when it is fair. 'Lord,' says David, 'in trouble they visited thee, they poured out a prayer when thy chastening was upon them.'

Nor would we intimate that none truly repent of their sins and obtain forgiveness, under such circumstances. Though late repentance is seldom genuine, yet, as Mr. Jay remarks, genuine repentance is never too late. God can pardon the sins of a century as easily as those of a day. Our friend was the means, in the hand of God, of leading many, when worn by sickness and at the eleventh hour of life, to the Lamb of God. His carefully kept diary records many such instances. We give one. He says, 'I remember one Sunday coming from Hessle with the Rev. C. Jones. Our "hearts burned within us as we talked by the way," and when we got to Coultam Street, a number of well-dressed young men overheard our conversation, and began to shout after us and call us approbrious names. Mr. J. talked with them, but to no purpose. Four months after, Mr. Jones and myself went, as usual, to visit the inmates of the infirmary; Mr. J. took one side and I the other, and when I came to a person who needed special counsel and advice, I used to call my friend to my aid. Well, we met with a young man who burst into a flood of tears, and casting an imploring look towards Mr. Jones, he said, "O sir, do forgive me." "Forgive you what?" said Mr. J. "what have you done that you should ask *me* to forgive you?" "Sir," said he, "I am one of those young men who were so impertinent to you one Sunday when you were returning from Hessle; do forgive me, sir." "I freely forgive you," replied my friend, "you must ask God to forgive you, for it is against him you have sinned." We then prayed with him, and asked God to forgive him. He was suffering from a broken leg, and I often used to visit him after our first interview. He obtained pardon, and rejoiced in Christ as his Saviour. He was a brand plucked from the burning.'

But Mr. Ellerthorpe also tells us that though he visited, during twenty-five years, hundreds of persons who cried aloud for mercy and professed to obtain forgiveness, on what was feared would be their dying beds, yet, he did not remember more than five or six who, on being restored to health, lived so as to prove their conversion genuine. The rest returned 'like the dog to its vomit, and the sow that was washed to her wallowing in the mire.' The Sabbath-breaker forgot his vows and promises, and returned to his Sunday pleasures. The swearer allowed his tongue to move as unchecked in insulting his Maker as before. The drunkard thirsted for his intoxicating cups and returned to the scenes of his former dissipations; and the profligate, who avowed himself a 'changed man,' when health was fully restored, laughed at religion as a fancy, and hastened to wallow in the mire of pollution. He had scarcely a particle of faith in sick-bed repentances, but believed that in most instances they are solemn farces.

Deeply affecting and admonitory are some of the instances he records. He says, 'One night an engineer called me out of bed to visit his wife, who was attacked with cholera. While I was praying with *her*, *he* was seized with the complaint. I visited them again the next day, when the woman died, but the husband, after a long affliction, recovered. He seemed sincerely penitent and made great promises of amendment. But, alas! like hundreds more whom I visited, he no sooner recovered, than he sought to shun me. At length he left the part of the town where he resided when I first visited him, as he said, "*to get out of my way.*" But at that time, I visited in all parts of the town, and I often met him, and it used to pain me to see the dodges he had recourse to in order to avoid meeting me in the street.'

He also records the case of a carter who resided in Collier Street. He was attacked with small pox, and was horrible to look at and infectious to come near, but being urged to visit him, 'I went to see him daily for a long time,' says John. 'One day when I called I found him, his wife, and child bathed in tears, for the doctor had just told them that the husband and father would be dead in a few hours. We all prayed that God would spare him, and spared he was. I continued to visit him thrice a day, and he promised that he would accompany me to class when he got better. At that time he seemed as though he would have had me ever with him. One day, as I entered his room, he said, "O Mr. Ellerthorpe, how I love to hear your foot coming into my house." I replied, 'Do you think it possible that there will come a time when you will rather see any one's face and hear any one's voice than mine?' "Never, no never," was his reply. I answered, 'Well, I wish and hope it may never happen as I have supposed.' Now, what followed? He went once to class, but I could not attend that night, having to watch the tide, and he never went again. I have seen him in the streets when he would go anywhere, or turn down any passage, rather than meet me; and when compelled to meet me he would look up at the sky or survey the chimney tops *rather* than see me.'

'On one occasion, when visiting at the Infirmary, going from ward to ward, and from bed to bed, I met with a young man, S. B——. He was very bad, and was afraid he was going to die. I talked with him often and long, pointing him to the Saviour, and prayed with him. With penitential tears and earnest cries he sought mercy, and at length professed to obtain salvation. He recovered. One Sunday, when at Hessle, visiting my dying mother, I met this young man, and I shall never forget his agitated frame, and terrified appearance, when he saw me. He looked this way and that way; I said, 'Well, B——, are you all right? Have you kept the promises you made to the Lord?' A blush of shame covered his face. I said 'Why do you look so sad? Have I injured you?' 'No, Sir.' 'Have you injured me?' 'I hope not,' was his reply. 'Then look me in the face; are you beyond God's reach, or do you think that because he has restored your health once, he will not afflict you again? Ah! my boy, the next time may be much worse than the last. And do you think God will believe you if you again promise to serve him? He looked round him and seemed as though he would have leaped over a drain that was close by.'

Conscience is a busy power within the breast of the most desperate, and when roused by the prospect of death and judgment, it speaks in terrible tones. The notorious Muller denied the murder of Mr. Briggs, until, with cap on his face and the rope round his neck, he submitted to the final appeal and acknowledged, as he launched into eternity, 'Yes, I have done it.' But the cries of these persons seem to have arisen, not from an abhorrence of sin, but from a dread of punishment; they feared hell, and hence they wished for heaven; they desired to be saved from the consequences of sin, but were not delivered from the love of it. Need we wonder that our friend had but little faith in a sick-bed repentance? Scripture and reason alike warn us against trusting to such repentance, 'Be not deceived; God is not mocked: for whatsoever a man soweth, that shall he also reap. For he that soweth to the flesh shall of the flesh reap corruption; but he that soweth to the Spirit shall of the Spirit reap life everlasting.'

While our friend felt that he would have been unworthy the name of a Christian had he not felt more for the spiritual than for the temporal woes of his fellow creatures, yet the latter were not forgotten by him; and it sometimes grieved him that he could not more largely minister to the temporal wants of the poor, the fatherless, the orphans, and the widows, whom he visited

And perhaps one of the most painful trials a visitor of the sick endures is, to go moneyless to a chamber that has been crossed by want, and whose inmate is utterly unable to supply his own necessities; but when the visitor can relieve the physical as well as the spiritual necessities of the sufferer, with what a buoyant step and cheerful heart he enters the abode of poverty and suffering! And his words, instead of falling like icicles on the sufferer's soul, fall on it as refreshing as a summer rain, warm as the tempered ray, and welcome as a mother's love. Such a visitor has often chased despair from the abode of wretchedness, and filled it with the atmosphere of hope.

Hence, that he might participate in this joy, and have wherewith to relieve the needy, Mr. Ellerthorpe abstained from the use of tobacco, of which, at one period of his life, he was an immoderate consumer. One Sabbath morning, while he and Mr. Harrison were visiting the sick, they met two wretched-looking boys, fearfully marked with small pox (from an attack of which complaint they were beginning to recover), and crying for a drink of milk. Their father, who was far advanced in life, could not supply their wants. John's heart was touched, and he thought, 'Here am I, possessed of health, food, and raiment, while these poor children are festering with disease, but scantily clothed, and not half fed. A sixpence, a basin of milk, or a loaf of bread, would be a boon to them. Can I help them?' He gave the old man sixpence, while he and Mr. Harrison told the milkman to leave a quantity of milk at the man's house daily, for which they would pay. It was with a radiant face, and a tremble of glad emotion in his voice, that our friend, in relating this circumstance to us one day, said:—I felt a throb of pleasure when I did that little act of kindness, such as I had never felt before,' when, quick as lightning, the thought crossed his mind, 'Why I smoke six pennyworth of tobacco every week!' and there and then he resolved to give up the practice. On the next Friday, when Mrs. Ellerthorpe was setting down on paper a list of the groceries wanted, she proceeded, as usual, to say, 'Tea—Coffee—Sugar—*Tobacco*—,' 'Stop,' said her husband, 'I've done with that. I'll have no more.' Now, Mrs. E. had always enjoyed seeing her husband smoke; it had often proved a powerful sedative to him when wearied with the cares of life, and the numberless irritations of his trying vocation, and therefore she replied, 'Nonsense, you will soon repent of that whim. I shall get two ounces as usual, and I know you'll smoke it.' 'I shall never touch it again,' was his firm reply, and ever after kept his word.

A world full of misery, both temporal and spiritual, surrounds us, and which might be effectually relieved, were all Christians, many of whom are laggard in effort and niggard in bounty, to manifest a tithe of the self-denial which Mr. Ellerthorpe practiced. 'What maintains one vice, would support two children.' Robert Hall says:—It is the practice of self-denial in a thousand little instances which forms the truest test of character.' Mr. Fletcher, Vicar of Madeley, was on one occasion driven close for means to discharge the claims of the poor, when he said to his wife, 'O Polly, can we not do without beer? Let us drink water, and eat less meat. Let our necessities give way to the extremities of the poor.' And at a meeting held the other night, a donation was announced thus:—'A poor man's savings from tobacco, £5.' And are there not tens of thousands of professors who could present similar offerings if they, in the name and spirit of their great Master, tried? Do we not often come in contact with men who complain that they cannot contribute to the cause of God and humanity, who, at the same time, indulge in the use of snuff, tobacco, or intoxicating drinks; all of which might be laid aside to the gain of God's cause, and without at all lessening either the health, reputation, or happiness of the consumer? And are there not others, of good social position, who do not give as much to relieve the temporal sufferings of their fellow creatures, during twelve months, as it costs them to provide a single feast for a few well-to-do friends? The merchant who sold his chips and shavings, and presented the proceeds to the cause of God, while he kept the solid timber for himself, is the type of too many professors of religion!

CHAPTER IV.

HIS STAUNCH TEETOTALISM.

PERHAPS no class of men have suffered more from the evils of intemperane than our brave sailors, fishermen, and rivermen. Foreigners tell our missionaries to convert our drunken sailors abroad, and when they wish to personify an Englishman, they mockingly reel about like a drunken man. And what lives have been lost through the intemperance of captains and crews! The 'St. George,' with 550 men: 'The Kent,' 'East Indiaman,' with most of her passengers and crew: 'The Ajax,' with 350 people: 'The Rothsway Castle,' with 100 men on board, with many others we might name, were all lost through the drunkenness of those in charge of the vessels.' Of the forty persons whom our friend rescued from drowning, a very large percentage got overboard through intemperance. We read that on the morning following the Passover night in Egypt, there was not a house in which there was not one dead, and it would be difficult to find a house in our land, occupied by sailors, in which this monster evil has not slain its victim, either physically or morally.

Our friend, speaking of his own family, says:—'I owe my Christian name to the favour with which drunkenness was regarded by my relatives. Soon after I was born, one of my uncles asked, 'What is the lad's name to be?'" "Thomas," replied my, mother. "Never," said my uncle, in surprise, "we had two Thomas's, and they both did badly; call him John. I have known four John's in the family, and they *were all great drunkards, but that was the worst that could be said of them.*" 'So it appears,' said our friend, 'that at that time it was thought no very bad thing for a man to get drunk, if he was not in the habit of being brought before the magistrate for theft, &c.' John's father was one of the four drunkards. In early life he became a hard drinker, and he continued the practice until a damaged constitution, emptied purse, a careworn wife, and a neglected family, were the bitter fruits of his inebriation. 'He drank hard,' says John, 'spending almost all his money in drink, and was at last forced to sell his vessel and take to the menial work of helping to load and unload vessels. At length he went to sea, and for a long time we heard nothing of him; nor did my mother receive any money from him. In old age he was quite destitute, and while it gave me great pleasure to minister to his necessities, it often grieved me to think of the cause of his altered circumstances.'

Nightly, when ashore, John, the elder, went to the public house, and it was his invariable rule never to return home until his wife fetched him. Often, when Mrs. Ellerthorpe was in a feeble state of health, and amid the howling winds and drenching rains of a winter's night, would she go in search of her drunken husband, and by her winning ways and kind entreaties induce him to return home. She was known to be a God-fearing woman, and often on the occasion of these visits, her husband's companions— some of whom were 'tippling professors' of religion—would try to entangle her in religious conversation, but to every entreaty she had one reply, 'If you want to talk with me about religion come to my house. I will not speak of it here; for I am determined never to fight the devil on his own ground.'

And was this Christian woman wrong in calling the public house the devil's ground? We have 140,000 of these houses in our land, and are they not so many reservoirs from whence the devil floods our country with crime, wretchedness, and woe? Is it not there that his deluded victims, in thousands of instances, destroy their fortune, ruin their health, and form those habits which wither the beauty, scatter the comforts, blast the reputation, and bury once happy families in the tomb of disgrace? And is it not at the public house that the sounds of blasphemy, cursing, and swearing, sedition, uncleanness, laciviousness, hatred, quarrels, murders, gambling, revelling, and such like, are begun? And you might as reasonably expect to preserve your health in a pest-house, your modesty in a brothel, and high-souled principles amongst gamesters, as to expect to preserve your religious character undamaged amid the impure atmosphere of a public house. Can a man go upon hot coals and his feet not be burnt? One hour spent around the drunkard's table has often done an amount of harm to the cause of God and the souls of men which the devotion of years could not undo.

A youth, on being urged to take the pledge, said, 'My father drinks, and I don't want to be better than my father.' And, alas! for our friend, he early imbibed the tastes and followed the example of his father, for drink got the mastery of him. Speaking of his boyhood, he says, 'I remember a man saying to my father, " Your son is a sharp lad, and he will make a clever man, if only you set him a good example, and keep him from drink." To which my father replied, "O drink will not hurt him; if he does nothing worse than take a sup of drink he'll be all right; drink never hurt anyone." But, alas! my father lived to see that a "little sup" did not serve me, for I have heard him say with sorrow, "The lad drinks hard." But he was the first to set me the example, and if parents wish their children to abstain from intoxicating drinks, they should set the example by being abstainers themselves. The best and most lasting way of doing good to a family is for parents first to do right themselves.' But with such a training as John had, what wonder that he became a 'hard drinker.' For years previous to his marriage his experience was something like that of an old 'hard-a-weather' on board a homeward-bound Indiaman, who was asked by a lady passenger, 'Whether he would not be glad to get home and see his wife and children, and spend the summer with them in the country?' Poor Jack possessed neither home, nor wife, nor chick nor child; and his recollections of green fields and domestic enjoyments were dreamily associated with early childhood. And hence a big tear rolled down his weather-beaten but manly cheek as he said to his fair questioner, 'Well, I don't know, I suppose it will be another *roll in the gutter, and away again.*' Our friend was for years a 'reeling drunkard,' and often, during this sad period of his existence, he literally 'rolled in the gutter.'

But when he experienced a saving change he at once became a sober man, and began to treat public houses after the fashion of the fox in the fable—who declined the invitation to the lion's den, because he had observed that the only footsteps in its vicinity were towards it and none from it. He further saw that to indulge in the use of intoxicating drinks, and then pray, 'Lead me not into temptation,' savoured less of piety than of presumption. He attended a temperance meeting at which the Rev. G. Lamb spoke of the importance of Christian professors abstaining for the good of others, as well as for their own safety. John felt that his sphere of action was limited in its range and insignificant in its character; yet he knew he possessed influence; as a husband and father, and as a member of civil and religious society, he knew that his conduct would produce an effect on those to whom he was related, and with whom he had to do. 'No man liveth to himself.' He knew how to do good, and not to have done it would have been sin. And that thought decided him. At the close of the meeting, persons were invited to take the pledge of total abstinence, but not one responded to the invitation. John saw, sitting at his right hand, a man who had been a great drunkard, and whose shattered nerves, unsteady hand, and bloodshot eyes, told of the sad effects of his conduct. Placing his hand on this man's shoulder, he said, 'Will you take the pledge?' 'I will if you will,' was the man's reply. 'Done,' said John, and scarcely had they reached the platform, when about twenty others followed and took the pledge.

His Diary contains this record, 'February 24th, 1851. I have been to the Teetotal Meeting, and I have taken the pledge, and I intend, through the grace of God, to keep it as long as I live.'

From that night John became a practical and pledged abstainer from all intoxicating drinks, and induced many a poor drunkard to follow his example. No man stood higher than he in Temperance circles. He adorned *that* profession. In his extensive intercourse with his fellow men, he proved himself the fast friend and unflinching advocate of total abstinence, having delivered hundreds of addresses and circulated thousands of tracts, in vindication of its principles.

A few years before his death, he was travelling from Hull to Howden, by rail; the compartment was full of passengers, and he began, as usual, to circulate his tracts and to speak in favour of temperance.

An aged clergyman present said, 'I always give you Hull folks great credit for being teetotalers.' 'And why the people of Hull more than the people of any other place?' asked John. 'Because your water is filthy and dirty, and I never could drink it without a mixture of brandy.' 'That our water is dirty I admit,' said John, 'but I have drank it both with brandy and without, and if you felt as I feel, I am sure, sir, you would discontinue the practice of brandy drinking.' 'Oh, I suppose you are one of those men who get all the drink you can and when you can get no more you turn teetotaller,' was the rejoinder. 'You are mistaken, sir; for I can call most of the persons present to witness, that I laid aside the intoxicating glass when I possessed the most ample means and every opportunity of getting plenty of drink, and at little or no cost to myself. But I saw that I should be a safer and happier man myself, and a greater blessing to others if I abstained, and therefore I signed the pledge; and you must pardon me, sir, when I say, that if you felt as I feel, you would, as a minister of the gospel, pursue the same course.' 'O!' said he, with indignation lowering in his countenance and thundering in his voice, 'I have taken my brandy daily for years, and it never did me any hurt.' 'Granted,' replied our friend, 'but if you can drink with safety, can others? Have you never seen the evil effects of tampering with the glass? Have none of your acquaintances or friends fallen victims to drunkenness? Let me give you a case, sir. One of my former employers had a son who, up to the twentieth year of his age, had never tasted intoxicating drinks. But he had a weak constitution and a slender frame, and the doctor ordered him to take a little brandy and water twice a day. He did so, and began to like it. He soon wanted it oftener, and told the man to make it stronger, and the man did as he was told. One day he had put but a few drops of water into a large glass of brandy, but the young gentleman said, 'Did'nt I tell you to make it stronger? Let the next glass be stronger.' He soon called *for the next glass*, and having swallowed it, said, in a rage, 'What a fool you are. I told you to let me have it stronger.' 'Sir,' said the man, 'you can't have it stronger, for the glass you have just drank was "neat" as it came from the bottle.' 'And is that a fact,' exclaimed the young gentleman. 'Has it come to this? Am I to be a slave to that liquid? Never! Take it away, and from this day I'll never drink another glass.' This statement was listened to with marked attention by all the passengers, and when the train arrived at Howden station, they gave forth a spontaneous burst of applause. The clergyman sat ashamed and speechless, and, on leaving the train, refused to shake hands with our friend who had administered to him this well-timed and well-merited rebuke.

I have stated that our friend spoke at hundreds of temperance meetings, and his bluntness of manner, curt style of address, and nautical phrases, won for him a ready hearing. Whenever he rose on the platform eyes beamed and hearts throbbed with delight. Not that his hearers expected to listen to an eloquent speech, or to be amused by laughter-exciting and fun-making eccentricities, but he rose with the influence of established character, combined with an ardent temperament, a ready wit, and a face beaming with the sunshine of piety towards God and good-will to men. Besides, there was a just appreciation of his many deeds of gallantry, some of which he occasionally related, and which rarely failed to fill his hearers with admiration for the brave heart that could prompt and the ready skill that could perform them. Hence, he was listened to in the town and neighbourhood of Hull with an amount of sympathy, attention, and respect which no other advocate of total abstinence, possessed of the same mental abilities, could command.

The *Band of Hope* had a warm friend and powerful advocate in the person of Mr. Ellerthorpe, and it was in connexion with its services that he found his most congenial employment. 3,000,000 of the inhabitants of our country are now pledged abstainers from intoxicating drinks, and this number includes upwards of 2,000 ministers of the Gospel. But thirty years ago this cause was regarded with disfavour even by the religious public. Hence, when Mr. Ellerthorpe and others sought to form a Band of Hope in connexion with the Primitive Methodist Sabbath School, Great Thornton Street, Hull, they met with much opposition from several members of the Society, and also from some of the teachers in the school, who were 'tipplers,' and could not endure the idea of a Band of Hope. But the Band was formed, with Mr. Ellerthorpe as president, and it soon numbered three hundred members. Before his death he saw upwards of thirty of these Juvenile Bands formed in Hull. He attended most of their anniversaries, throwing a flood of genial merriment, just like dancing sunlight, over his young auditors. Hundreds of these 'cold water drinkers' sometimes listened to him on these occasions, and as he related some of the scenes of his eventful life, their young hearts throbbed and their eyes filled with tears.

We cannot close this chapter of our little book without asking, Were the motives which led our friend to sign the pledge, right or wrong? The celebrated Paley lays down this axiom, 'That where one side is doubtful and one is safe, we are as morally bound to take the safe side as if a voice from heaven said, "This is the way, walk ye in it."' And is not total abstinence the only safe side for the abstainer himself? Some men have a strong predisposition for intoxicating drinks, and they must abstain or be ruined. Naturalists tell us that in order to tame a tiger he must never be allowed to taste blood. Let him have but one taste and his whole nature is changed. And the men to whom I refer are humane, upright, chaste, kind to their children and affectionate to their wives, while they can be kept from intoxicating drinks, but let them taste, only *taste*, and their passions become so strong and their appetites so rampant, that they are inspired with the most ferocious dispositions, and perpetrate deeds, the mere mention of which would appal them in their sober moments. And where is the moderate drinker who can point to the glass and say, 'I am safe?' As that dexterous murderer, Palmer, administered his doses in small quantities, and thus gradually and daily undermined the constitution of his victims, and, as it were, muffled the footfalls of death, so strong drink does not all at once over master its victims; but how often have we known it gradually, and after years of tippling, lead them captive into the vortex of drunkenness.

But admitting, for the sake of argument, that you can drink with safety to yourself, can you drink with safety to others? 'No man liveth to himself.' We are all a kind of chameleon, and naturally derive a tinge from that which is near us. Our friend attributes his early drunkenness to the influence and example of his father. You should view your drinking habits in the light of these passages of Scripture, 'Look not every man on his own things, but every man also on the things of others.' 'It is good neither to eat flesh, nor to drink wine, nor anything whereat thy brother stumbleth or is made weak.' So that you may look at Paley's saying, in its application to the use of strong drinks, again and again; you may examine it as closely as you like, and criticise it as often as you please, still it remains true, that to drink is *doubtful*, while to abstain is *safe*, and that we are as morally bound to choose the latter as if a voice from heaven said, 'This is the way, walk ye in it.' 'Let us not, therefore, judge one another any more, but judge this rather that no man put a stumblingblock or an occasion to fall in his brother's way.'—Rom. xiv. 13.

CHAPTER V.

HIS BOLD ADVENTURES ON THE WATER.

THAT swimming is a noble and useful art, deserving the best attention of all classes of the community, is a fact few will dispute. 'Swimming,' says Locke, 'ought to form part of every boy's education!' It is an art that is easily acquired; it is healthy and pleasurable as an exercise, being highly favourable to muscular development, agility of motion, and symmetry of form; and it is of inconceivable benefit as the means of preserving or saving life in seasons of peril, when death would otherwise prove inevitable. Mr. Ellerthorpe early became an accomplished swimmer; he often fell overboard, and but for his skill in the art under consideration he would have been drowned. He also enjoyed the happiness of having saved upwards of forty persons, who, but for his efforts must, to all human appearance, have perished.

To a maratime nation like ours, with a rugged and dangerous coast-line of two thousand miles, indented by harbours, few and far from each other, and with a sea-faring population of half a million, it seems as necessary that the rising generation should learn to swim as that they should be taught the most common exercises of youth. And yet 'this nata'ory art' is but little cultivated amongst us. On the Continent, and among foreigners generally, swimming is practised and encouraged far more than it is in England. In the Normal Swimming school of Denmark, some thirty years ago, there were educated 105 masters destined to teach the art throughout the kingdom. In France, Vienna, Copenhagen, Stockholm. Berne, Amsterdam, &c., similar means were adopted, and very few persons in those countries are entirely destitute of a knowledge of the art. But so generally is this department of juvenile training neglected by us as a people, that *only one in every ten who gain their livelihood on the water* are able to swim.

Mr. Ellerthorpe, in a characteristic letter, says: 'I think no schoolmaster should regard the education of his scholars complete unless he has taught them to swim. That art is of service when everything else is useless. I once heard of a professor who was being ferried across a river by a boatman, who was no scholar. So the professor said, "Can you write, my man?" "No, Sir," said the boatmam. "Then you have lost one third of your life," said the professor. "Can you read?" again asked he of the boatman. "No," replied the latter, "I can't read." "Then you have lost the half of your life," said the professor. Now came the boatman's turn. "Can you swim?" said the boatman to the professor. "No," was his reply. "Then," said the boatman, "you have lost the whole of your life, for the boat is sinking and you'll be drowned." Now, Sir, I think that if those fathers who spend so much money on the intellectual education of their children, would devote but a small portion of it to securing for them a knowledge of the art of swimming, they would confer a great blessing on those children, and also on society at large I would have every one learn to swim females as well as males; for many of both sexes come under my notice every year who are drowned, but who, with a little skill in swimming, might have been saved. Not fewer than forty men and boys were lost from the Hull Smacks alone during the year 1866, of whom twenty per cent. might have been saved had they been able to swim.'

Mr. Ellerthorpe was, for many years, Master of the 'Hull Swimming Club,' and also of 'The College Youth's Swimming Club,' and his whole life was a practical lesson on the value of the art of swimming. He contended that the youths of Hull ought to be taught this art, and pleaded that a sheet of water which had been waste and unproductive for twenty years should be transformed into a swimming bath.

The local papers favoured the scheme, and Alderman Dennison, moved in the Town Council, that £350 should be devoted to this object, which was carried by a majority. The late Titus Salt, Esq., who had given £5,000 to the 'Sailor's Orphan Home,' said at the time, 'I think *your corporation ought to make the swimming bath* alluded to in the enclosed paper; *do ask them.*' 'The private individual who gives his *fifty* hundreds to a particular Institution,' to use the words of the *Hull and Eastern Counties' Herald, Oct.* 10th, 1857, 'has surely a right to express an opinion that the municipal corporation ought to grant *three* hundreds, if by so doing the public weal would be provided. If the voice of such a man is to be disregarded, then it may truly be said that our good old town has fallen far below the exalted position it occupied when it produced its WILBERFORCE and its MARVEL.'

For upwards of forty years Mr. Ellerthorpe was known as a fearless swimmer and diver, and during that period he saved no fewer than forty lives by his daring intrepidity. In his boyhood, he, to use his own expression, '*felt quite at home in the water,*' and betook himself to it as natively and instinctively as the swan to the water or the lark to the sky. 'This art,' to use the words of an admirable article in the *Shipwrecked Mariners' Magazine* for October, 1862, 'he has cultivated so successfully that in scores of instances he has been able to employ it for the salvation of life and property. Perhaps the history of no other living person more fully displays the value of this art than John Ellerthorpe. Joined with courage, promptitude, and steady self possession, it has enabled him repeatedly to preserve his own life, and what is far more worthy of record, to save not fewer than thirty-nine of his fellow creatures, who, humanly speaking, must otherwise have met with a watery grave.'

It is but right to state that, in the early period of his history, a thoughtless disregard of his own life, and an overweening confidence in his ability to swim almost any length, and amid circumstances of great peril, often led him to deeds of 'reckless daring,' which in riper years he would have trembled to attempt. Respecting most of the following circumstances he says, 'I look upon those perilous adventures as so many foolish and wicked temptings of Providence. I have often wondered I was not drowned, and attribute my preservation to the wonder-working providence of God, who has so often 'redeemed my life from destruction, and crowned me with loving kindness and tender mercies.'

And certainly we should remember that heroism is one thing, reckless daring another. Two or three instances will illustrate this. A few years ago Blondin, for the sake of money, jeopardized his life at the Crystal Palace, by walking blindfolded on a tight-rope, and holding in his hand a balancing pole. In so doing he was foolhardy, but not heroic. But a certain Frenchman, at Alencon, walked on one occasion on a rope over some burning beams into a burning house, otherwise inaccessible, and succeeded in saving six persons. This was the act of a true hero. When Mr. Worthington, the 'professional diver,' plunged into the water and saved six persons from drowning, who, but for his skill and dexterity as a swimmer, would certainly have met with a watery grave, he acted the part of a 'hero;' but when, the other day, he made a series of nine 'terrific plunges' from the Chain Pier at Brighton—a height of about one hundred and twenty feet—merely to gratify sensational sightseers, or to put a few shillings into his own pocket, he acted the part of a foolhardy man. Can we wonder that he was within an ace of losing his life in this mad exploit? And when John Ellerthorpe dived to the bottom of 'Clarke's Bit,' to gratify a number of young men who had 'more money than wit,' and struggled in the water with a bag of coals on his back, he put himself on a par with those men who place their lives in imminent danger by dancing on ropes, swinging on cords, tying themselves into knots like a beast, or crawling on ceilings like some creeping thing! But when he used his skill to save his fellow creatures, he was a true hero, and was justified in perilling his own life, considering that by so doing the safety of others might be secured.

We shall close this chapter by recording a few of his deeds of reckless daring.

'My first attempt at swimming took place at Hessle, when I was about twelve years of age. There was a large drain used for the purpose of receiving the water from both the sea and land. My father managed the sluice, which was used for excluding, retaining, and regulating the flow of water into this drain. It was a first rate place for lads to bathe in, and I have sometimes bathed in it ten times a day; indeed, I regret to say, I spent many days there when I ought to have been at school. I soon got to swim in this drain, but durst not venture into the harbour. But one day I accidentally set my dirty feet upon the shirt of a boy, who was much older and bigger than myself, and in a rage he took me up in his arms and threw me into the harbour. I soon felt safe there, nor did I leave the harbour till I had crossed and recrossed it thirty-two times. The next day I swam the whole length of the harbour twice, and from that day I began to match myself with expert swimmers, nor did I fear swimming with the best of them. Some other lads were as venturesome as myself, and we used to go up the Humber with the tides, for several miles at once. I remember on one occasion it blew a strong gale of wind from S.W., several vessels sank in the Humber, and a number of boats broke adrift, while a heavy sea was running: I stripped and swam to one of the boats, got into her, and brought her to land, for which act the master of the boat gave me five shillings. During the same gale a keel came ashore at Hessle; I stripped and swam to her and brought a rope on shore, by the assistance of which, two men, a woman, and two children escaped from the vessel. The tide was receding at the time, so that they were enabled, with the assistance of the rope, to walk ashore. There are several old men living now who well remember this circumstance.

'Soon after this occurrence, I remember one Saturday afternoon, going with some other boys of my own age, and swimming across the Humber, a distance of two miles. We started from Swanland Fields (which was then enclosed), Yorkshire, and landed at the Old Warp, Lincolnshire. Here we had a long run and a good play, and then we recrossed the Humber. But in doing so we were carried up as far as Ferriby Sluice, and had to run back to where we had left our clothes in charge of some lads, but when we got there the lads had gone, and we didn't know what to do. We sought for our clothes a full hour, when a man, in the employ of Mr. Pease told us that the lads had put them under some bushes, where we at last found them. We were in the water four hours. This was an act of great imprudence.

'On another occasion myself and some other lads played truant from school, and went towards the Humber to bathe, but the schoolmaster, Mr. Peacock, followed us closely. He ran and I ran, and I had just time to throw off my clothes and leap into the water, when he got to the bank. He was afraid I should be drowned, and called out 'If you will come back I won't tell your father and mother.' But I refused to return, for at that time I felt no fear in doing what I durst not have attempted when I got older.

'On several occasions some young gentlemen, who were scholars at Hessle boarding school, got me to go and bathe with them. They had plenty of money, and I had none; and as they offered to pay me, I was glad to go with them. One day while we were bathing, the eldest son of Mr. Earnshaw, of Hessle, had a narrow escape from drowning. I was a long way from him at the time, but I did all I could to reach and rescue him. He was very ill for some days, and the doctor forbade him bathing for a long time to come. This deterred us from bathing for awhile, but we soon forgot it. We agreed to have a swimming match, and the boy that swam the farthest was to have *sixpence*. We started at three o'clock in the afternoon from the third jetty below Hessle harbour, and went up with the tide. One of the boys got the lead of me and I could not overtake him until we got opposite Cliffe Mill, about a mile and a half from where we started. He then began to fag, while I felt as brisk as a lark and fresher than when I began. I soon took the lead, and when I got to Ferriby Lane-end, I lost my mate altogether. However, I knew he was a capital swimmer, and I felt afraid lest he should turn up again, so I swam as far as Melton brickyard, and fairly won the prize. I had swam about seven miles, and believe I could have swam back without landing.

'When I was about fifteen years of age a steam packet came to Hessle, bringing a number of swimmers from Hull. Soon after their arrival a lad came running to me and said, "Jack, there's some of those Hull chaps bathing, and they say they can beat thee." I didn't like that; and when I got to them, a young gentleman said, pointing to me, "Here is a lad that shall swim you for what you like." One of them said, "Is he that Ellerthorpe of Hessle?" "No matter who he is," replied the young man, "I'll back him for a sovereign," when one of the young gentlemen called out, "It is Jack Ellerthorpe, I won't have aught to do with him, for he can go as fast feet foremost as I can with my hands foremost, he's a first-rate swimmer." By this time I was stripped, and at once plunged into the river. I crept on my hands and knees on the water, and then swam backwards and forwards with my feet foremost, and not one among them could swim with me. I showed them the "porpoise race," which consisted in disappearing under the water, and then coming "bobbing" up suddenly, at very unlikely spots. I then took a knife and cut my toe-nails in the water. The young gents were greatly delighted, and afterwards they would have matched me to swim anybody, to any distance. And I believe that at that time I could have swam almost any length; for after I had swam two or three miles my spirits seemed to rise, and my strength increased. When other lads seemed thoroughly beaten out, I was coming to my best, and the longer I remained in the water the easier and faster I could swim.

'It will be remembered by some who will read these pages, that about . . . . years ago a Mr. Burton was returned, as a member of Parliament for Beverley. He was a wild, drunken, half-crazy fellow, and I remember he came to Hessle about two o'clock one afternoon, and drove full gallop, with postillions, up to my father's house. At that time my father was ferryman, and Mr. Burton wanted a boat to take him to Barton. "But," said my father, "there is no water," when the Member of Parliament said, "Won't money make the boat swim?" "I'm afraid not," was my father's reply. At that time, however, there was a ballast lighter at Cliffe, and my father and I went to see if we could borrow the lighter's boat; we succeeded, and as it was a great distance from the water (the tide being low), my father asked the Cliffe men to help in launching it, when about thirty of them came to his assistance. Mr. Burton left a guinea to be spent in drink for the men. We then started in the boat, and took Mr. Burton to Barrow, there being no *usable* jetty at Barton. I was to run to Barton for a post-chaise, but before we got to the shore the boat ran aground, so out of the boat I jumped, and away I ran, until I came to a pool of water, about twelve feet deep. Almost mad with excitement, I sprang into it, and small as I was, soon crossed it and was ashore. Mr. Burton saw me in the water, and he was afraid I should be drowned, and when I returned with the chaise he gave me a sovereign, the first I ever had, so you may be sure I was mightily pleased. I found my father and the men drunk, and they gave me some rum. On being asked, "What Mr. Burton had given me," I evaded the question by saying "A shilling," for I was of opinion that if my father had known I had got so much as I had, he would have taken most of it to spend in drink. So I hastened home and gave the sovereign to my mother, and we were both highly delighted to possess so large a sum of money.

'The following amusing circumstance took place in 1836-7, when I belonged to the Barton and Hessle packet. One day we had put on board the "tow boat" a great number of fat beasts, belonging, if I remember rightly, to Mr. Wood, of South Dalton. The "tow boat" was attached to the steamer by a large thick rope. We had not got far from Barton when the boat capsized, and we were in an awful mess. The boat soon filled with water; some of the beasts swam one way and some another, while several got entangled in the rails attached to the boat's side, and were every moment in danger of breaking their legs. So seizing an axe I jumped into the water and cut away the rails, and then went in pursuit of the oxen, heading them round in the water and causing them, by shouts and gestures, to swim for the land. Most of them were driven back to Barton and landed safely, others swam across the Humber and were landed at Hessle. I was up to my chest in water and mud for nearly three hours swimming backwards and forwards after the beasts; sometimes I had hold of their tails, and anon had to meet them and turn them towards the shore. There are lots of people now living at Barton who saw the affray, and who could describe it much better than I have done.

'A similar incident took place in 1844. I was captain of a ferry-boat plying between Winteringham and Brough. One Sabbath-day I was taking a load of beasts from Brough to Winteringham, and when we had got about half way across the Humber, the boat upset, and the beasts were thrown into the water. I was afraid they all would be drowned, and, in spite of all I could do, some of them were. I jumped overboard and drove some of them back to Brough, while others swam to the Lincolnshire side of the river. I was swimming about after the beasts for five hours, chasing them backwards and forwards, turning them this way and that, and doing what nobody but myself would have done. At length, several men came to our assistance, and when we had got the poor animals out of the water, we hastened to the public-house at the harbour-side, and got drunk. I kept my wet clothes on until they dried on my back. This was one of the most wretched days of my life. My anxiety about the beasts, the exhaustion brought on by my efforts to get them safe to land, and the sense of misery and degradation I felt when I thought of the plight I was found in on the blessed Sabbath-day, I shall never forget.

'On one occasion I was helping to load the "Magna Charter," and being half drunk, I fell into Hull harbour, with upwards of eight stones of coal on my back, but through foolish bravado I refused to let the bag drop into the water. After being in the water several minutes, I swam to the landing with the coals on my back, amid the deafening shouts of scores of spectators I look back on this act of temerity with feelings of shame and unmixed regret.'

When sailing from Hull to Barton, one night in the year 1842, John was thrown overboard. The night was dark, the wind was blowing a heavy gale from the west, and every moment the spring-tide, then at its height, carried him further from the packet, which soon became unmanageable. The boat was launched, but the engineer, who had charge of it, became greatly agitated and much alarmed, and uttered the most piteous cries. 'I felt more for him than I did for myself,' says John, 'and though one moment lost in the trough of the sea, and the next on the crest of the billows, now near the boat and again fifty yards from it, I cried out, 'Scull away, Bob, scull away, thou'll soon be at me' After being in the water half-an hour I reached the boat in safety. All this time I had on the following garments, made of very stout pilot-cloth: a pair of trousers, a double-breasted waistcoat, a surtout coat, and a heavy great-coat, which came down to my ancles, a thick shawl round my neck, and a new pair of Wellington boots on my feet. I had in my pockets the following sums of money: £25 in bank notes; 25 sovereigns; £4 16s. 6d in silver, and 8d in coppers; also a tobacco-box, a large pocket knife, and a silver watch and guard. I made an attempt to throw off some of my clothes, but the thought of losing another man's money checked me. Besides, the suit of clothes I had on was bran-new, and being a poor man, and only just earning a livelihood, I could not brook the thought of having to get a new "rigging." When a wave carried me a great way from the boat, I unbuttoned my coat and prepared to throw it off, that I might more easily swim to land And when it seemed certain I should have to make this attempt, I felt for my knife, that I might cut off my boots, and I believe I could have done it; but, after a desperate effort, I approached within a few yards of the boat. when I again buttoned my coat. I felt confident I could have reached the shore — a distance of one mile — had I been compelled to make the trial. My Wellington boots had nearly cost me my life, as they were heavy and difficult to swim in, and I never wore a pair after this fearful night.'

There is another department of the art now under consideration, in which our friend greatly excelled, namely, that of diving. There are few divers who do not feel a kind of exultation in their power over the element, and in their ability to move under the surface of the water with ease and pleasure. Half a century ago, diving was a difficult and dangerous art, demanding great skill and endurance; but modern science has given the professional diver an almost perfect accoutrement, by means of which he can literally walk down to the bottom of the sea, and telegraph for as much air as he requires. Hence, it has been utterly deprived of all dramatic element. Properly managed, the thing is as easy as going up in a balloon, or going down a coal pit; but our friend excelled in 'real naked diving.'

His first attempt at fetching anything from under water took place when he was about sixteen years of age. The vessel in which he then sailed was being painted at 'Clark's Bit,' Castleford, when John accidentally let his brush fall overboard, and it sank to the bottom. The Captain was furious for about an hour, when, having handed the lad another brush, he went into the town. John could not brook the hour's grumbling to which he had been subjected, and hence, scarcely had the Master left the vessel, when he threw off his clothes and dived to the bottom of the 'Bit,' a depth of twenty-six feet, and brought up the brush. He hastily put on his clothes, and when the

Master returned, John held up the brush, and with that comical twinkle of the eye and humorous expression of the countenance, so common with sailors, said, 'Here's your brush, Sir.' 'What brush?' asked the Master 'The brush I lost overboard an hour ago,' said John. 'That's a lie,' replied the Master, 'how could you get it?' 'I dived to the bottom and brought it up,' was the lad's response. Now Clark's Bit, in those days, was supposed to be of fabulous depth; indeed, the Master, using a common expression, said, 'You can't have fetched it up from the bottom, for there is no bottom to Clark's Bit.' John was unabashed by this charge of falsehood, and with honesty beaming in every feature of his face, he answered with untrembling tongue, as he handed the brush to the Master, 'Throw it in again, Sir, and I'll fetch it up.' The Master refused to test the lad's honesty at the risk of losing his brush. However, several witnesses came forward and declared they had seen him plunge into the water and bring up the brush. From that time John was famous in the neighbourhood, as a great diver.

'At the time of this occurrence,' he writes, 'a number of young gentlemen were being taught, at a school at Castleford, by the Rev. Mr. Barnes. They had plenty of money, and I had little enough, and they would often, for the sake of seeing me dive to the bottom of the "Bit," throw in a shilling, and sometimes half a-crown. To gratify them, and for the sake of money, I often dived to the bottom, and never, that I remember, without bringing up the money. I got at last that I would not go down for less than a shilling, and I have sometimes got as much as five shillings a day. I have dived to the bottom of Clark's Bit hundreds of times, and there are numbers of people at Castleford, at the present day (1868), who recollect these youthful exploits, which took place upwards of forty years ago. And I may add that, I have often had the impression that but for that paint-brush I should never have been the diver I afterwards became God overruled these foolish acts, for good, and what I did for mere pleasure and gain, prepared me to rescue property and human life in after years.'

We will mention one instance of his prowess in saving property, which is well worthy of being recorded 'The barque "Mulgrave Castle," says the writer of the article in the *Shipwrecked Mariners' Magazine*, 'laden with timber from the Baltic, was waterlogged in the Humber; there was in the cabin of the vessel a small box containing money and papers which the captain was anxious, if possible, to secure. Ellerthorpe dived into the cabin, groped his way round it, and after two or three attempts succeeded in bringing up the box and its contents' This was in the year 1835 The writer of this sketch received the fact from an eye witness.

CHAPTER VI.

HIS METHOD OF RESCUING THE DROWNING.

FOR acts of pure, unselfish daring, in rescuing human life, the annals of our friend need not shun comparison with those of any other man within Her Majesty's dominion. It appears that, amid his wicked and wayward career, he had a 'deep and unaccountable impression' that one part of his mission into the world was to save human life. Beyond dispute, one of the best swimmers of his time, he was never, after his boyhood, satisfied with swimming as a mere art. It was naught to him if it did not help to make his fellow men better, safer, and braver. It will be seen that the first person he rescued from drowning *was his own father*, and that event ever afterwards nerved him to do his best to save his fellow-creatures. Indeed the desire to rescue the drowning burnt in his soul with all the ardour of an absorbing passion. It was the spring of his ready thoughts; it controlled his feelings and guided his actions; it prompted him to face the greatest difficulties without the least fear, and when in the midst of the most threatening dangers, it enabled him to summon up a calmness and resolution that never failed.

The writer in *The Shipwrecked Mariners' Magazine* says, 'Ellerthorpe's exploits in saving life date from the year 1820, and from that time to the present it may be safely asserted that he has never *hesitated* to risk his own life to save that of a fellow-creature. The danger incurred in jumping overboard to rescue a drowning person is very great. Many expert swimmers shrink from it. Ellerthorpe has encountered this risk under almost every variety of circumstance. He has followed the drowning, unseen in the darkness of the night, in the depth of winter, under rafts of timber, under vessels at anchor or in docks, from great heights, and often to the bottom in great depths of water, and what is very remarkable, never in vain. *Fortuna fortes juvet* (fortune favours the brave), is an adage true in his case. He never risked his life to save another without success'

Even to an experienced swimmer and diver, like our friend, the task of saving a drowning person is not easy, and the grip and grapple of some of those whom he rescued, had well nigh proved a fatal embrace, and it was only by the utmost coolness, skill, bravery, and self-control that he escaped.

But he shall tell *his own* simple, noble tale. 'During the last forty-eight years I have done all that lay in my power to rescue my fellow-creatures, when in drowning circumstances. By night and by day, in darkness or in light, in winter or in summer, I was always ready to obey the summons when the cry, "a man overboard," fell on my ears. And I have had to rescue the drowning in widely different ways. Sometimes I seized them tightly by the right arm, and then, hold them at arm's length. soon reached the land. In some instances they seized me by my shoulder or arm, when, leaving hold of them, and, throwing both my hands into the water, I managed to reach the shore. In other instances I found them so exhausted that they were incapable of taking hold of me, and in these cases, I had to carry them as a mother would carry her child. And in two or three instances, I thought they were dead, and, with feelings easier imagined than expressed, I bore them up in my arms; when suddenly, and with great strength, they sprang upon my head, and oftener than once, under these circumstances, I was on the point of being drowned. Some of those whom I saved were much heaver and stronger than myself, and when they got hold of me I found it difficult, and sometimes impossible, to shake them off When I rescued Robert Brown, the night was pitchy dark, and for some time I could not see him; and when I got to him he clutched me in such a manner as to prevent my swimming. When I seized the young Woodman, I thought he was dead, but, after a few moments, he made a great spring at me, and clutched hold of my head in such a way as to prevent me swimming for some seconds. When pinioned closely, I generally adopted this plan, which proved to be the best under the circumstances:—I threw myself on my back and pushed the drowning person on before me, and in this way I managed to keep them up for a time, and with comparative ease to myself. I often said to persons in a drowning state, "Now, hold fast by me, and don't exert yourself, and I'll make you all right." It was not often I could persuade them to act thus, but whenever they could, they got upon me; for "a drowning person will catch at a straw." I believe I have fetched out of the water not fewer than fifty drowning persons, and, with scarce an exception, they tried to seize me, and thus rendered their deliverance a matter of great difficulty. In fact, it would be comparatively easy to fetch a drowning man out of water if he would just take hold of one's arm, and thus keep himself from sinking, and let one tow him ashore.

'In many instances, as will be seen, I had to run a great distance, and when almost out of breath, I have plunged into the water, and in that state had to struggle with those on the point of drowning. J remember that, on one occasion, when staying at a public house in America, the landlord came running into the room, and cried out, "a man overboard." I ran 200 yards, and on reaching the spot I was out of breath, when in I plunged, but soon found I could not stay under the water for more than a few seconds. The water was clear and fresh, with long grass at the bottom; but alas! I could not find the young man, and he was drowned. I arrived too late to be of any service, for it was found afterwards that he had pulled himself on the bottom of the river with the long grass to a distance of fifty yards from the spot where he fell in.

'My first object, after I had plunged into the water, was to catch a sight of the drowning person, and if I could once do that, I always felt confident I should soon have him in my grasp. It is a most difficult thing to search for a drowning person, especially in muddy water. I had to make this attempt again and again, and sometimes the fear has crept over me that my exertions would be in vain, when I made the most prodigious and exhausting efforts. And that I have never failed, in a single instance, is to me a source of great gratitude to God, "in whose hand my breath is, and whose are all my ways."'

'I remember once I had my leg crushed between our packet and the pier, and for some days after I could not walk without the aid of crutches. One day I got down to the South End, but soon felt tired, and returned home; but after a short rest, I again went to the pier, when I was told that, during my short absence, a cabman, named Sharpe, had fallen into the harbour and was drowned. I was filled with indescribable distress at the news, and said, "If I had been here I would have saved him, despite my broken leg At least I would have tried." A man, who professed to be a great swimmer, was present, and he answered. "O. I can swim as well as you can," when my muscles began to quiver, and my blood to throb, and I replied, in no very good temper, I assure you, "I dispute that, unless you mean now that I have my broken leg Why did'nt you try to save him?" I always felt that I would much rather have the satisfaction of having tried to save a drowning person and fail, than have the miserable satisfaction of shaking my head and shrugging my shoulders and saying. "Oh, I knew it would be of no use trying to save him; it was foolish to try" "I could have done it," never saved a drowning man. "I will try," has enabled me, under God, to save fifty of my fellow creatures.

' I do not wish to intimate that every man who sees a fellow creature drowning, ought to plunge into the water to rescue that person. Indeed, I have seen two or three instances where men, who could not swim themselves, have jumped into the water to save the drowning, and in every instance the consequences have nearly been fatal. Before a person makes such an attempt, he should have tested his own ability to swim. If he can float himself and believes he can save the drowning person, he ought to make the attempt, and God will help him. This is not mere theory, but what I have felt again and again. Ever after my conversion to God, I used to pray, when plunging into the water, "Lord help me," and knowing as I did, that prayer melts the heart and moves the arm of Jehovah, I felt confident he would help me;

and so he did; for I often, when in the water, felt a sweet consciousness that God was with me. He taught my hands to war with the waters, and my fingers to grasp my precious freight. When struggling with the boy Woodman, these words came forcibly into my mind, and I repeated them in the water:—

> "When all thy mercies, O my God,
> My rising soul surveys,
> Transported with the view, I'm lost
> In wonder, love, and praise."

'I always felt it my duty, after rescuing a drowning person, to go to the house of God at night, and return public thanks to the Almighty. Ministers in the town, and especially the Wesleyan ministers, have often returned thanks to God from the pulpit, on the following Sabbath. On the morning following the deliverance, I generally went to see the rescued person, and sought to improve the event by impressing their mind with the uncertainty of life and with the importance of being prepared for death.

'In the following list I have given, as far as my memory and knowledge enabled me, a true and faithful account of the persons whom I have rescued from drowning. Extracts from newspapers, and letters from the parties themselves, and also from many who were eye-witnesses of their deliverance, have been freely used. There are several whom I have, at different times, saved from a watery grave, not included in this list, but as these events produced but little impression on my mind at the time of their occurrence, and as I am utterly unable to give either the names of the parties, or the time when I saved them, I can make no reliable mention of them at present, *though I hope* to be able to do so at some future time. I sincerely believe, however, that if I had kept a strict account of all these deliverances, instead of having to record thirty-nine cases, I should have been able to have recorded upwards of fifty. I regret now that I did not keep such a record. Every now and then I meet with persons who greet me as their deliverer. Two young men have done so within the last four months. And very pleasant to my mind it is to meet a fellow creature whom I have been the means, in the hands of a wonder-working Providence, of saving from a watery grave. But all the cases mentioned in the following chapter, except William Earnshaw and Captain Clegg, have been signed by living witnesses, and most of them were reported in the local newspapers, at the time of their occurrence. Many of these persons are still living; some of them I see almost daily, and *they* can speak for themselves. If I have made a mistake in spelling their names, or in relating the time when, or the circumstances under which, I saved them, I shall be glad to be corrected. And if I have offered an unkind reflection on any of my fellow creatures, or recorded a boastful sentence respecting what my fellow townsmen have been pleased to call my "deeds of daring," I hope to be forgiven by God, whose I am and whom I serve. Finally: as a large circle of my friends are anxious to have a true record of all the lives I have saved, I shall be highly pleased if any whom I have rescued, but whose names I have not recorded, will send me a few lines that may add to the interest of this little book, should a second edition be called for.'

John Ellerthorpe

CHAPTER VII.

HIS GALLANT AND HUMANE CONDUCT IN RESCUING THE DROWNING.

First.—JOHN ELLERTHORPE.* (1820.)

He was my father, and I was not more than fourteen years of age when I saved him. At the time he managed the ferry boat from Hessle to Barton. It required two persons to conduct the boat across the Humber, and as it cost my father a shilling each time he employed a man to assist him across, he often took me with him instead of a man, and thus saved the shilling. One morning, he took Mr. Thompson, corn miller, to Barton, and engaged to fetch him back at night; and there was this agreement between them, that my father was to receive the fare whether Mr. T—— returned or not. He did not return that night, though we waited for him until nine o'clock. The snow was then thick on the ground, the wind was blowing strong, and the waves were beginning to rise high in the Humber, and I was sitting, half-asleep, at the corner of a comfortable hearth, before a bright fire, when my father called out, 'Come, my boy, we'll be off.' We were soon in the boat, but had not got many yards, when my father fell overboard. I remember crying out most piteously, 'Oh. my father is overboard,' when I instantly plunged into the water and soon had fast hold of him. He had sunk to the bottom, a depth of sixteen feet, for when he came up he was covered with mud. We came up close to the boat's side, and, making a tremendous spring, I got hold of the boat's gunnel, and after a few moments my father also got hold of it with both his hands. He was a heavy man, weighing about fifteen stones, and could not swim. I said to him, 'Now, father,

---

* Those marked with a star distinguish the cases for which **Mr. Ellerthorpe** received the special medal of the **Royal Humane Society.**

can you keep hold while I fetch the Hull horse-boatmen?' whom we had left at the water-side house, when he replied, 'Yes, but be very sharp, my lad.' I then swam to the house, and called out, 'My father is overboard;' and when I returned with the men, I was glad to hear him shout, 'I'm here.' John Thrush, captain of the horse-boat, and Luke Dixon, soon got him into the boat, while Mr. Wood, the landlord, brought him a glass of brandy, which he drank. We could not persuade him to leave the boat, so we again started for home, and as a brisk wind was blowing at the time, in about fifteen minutes, we were safe in Hessle harbour. My mother met us there, and I said, 'Mother, my father has been overboard, fetch somebody to help him out of the boat.' He was stiff and cold, but with the aid of Mr. Wright we got him ashore. Mr. W. brought him some mulled ale and a glass of rum, which I then thought very good. We then wrapped him in several thicknesses of warm clothing. I was much perished at the time, but soon felt all right. Not long before this, my mother had given me a severe flogging for bathing so often; so I looked into her face and said, 'Mother, I think you won't flog me for bathing again, will you?' to which she replied, 'Oh, my lad, it was a good job that thou was there;'* when my father faintly added, 'Yes, if he had not been there I should never have come to the top of the water.' And if he had he would have been drowned, for he could not swim a yard; and had he shouted, no one was near to render him assistance. But, thank God, I was there, and answered

---

* John seems to have loved his mother with a tender, intense affection. In a letter dated October 14th, 1867, he says: 'It is fourteen years this day since my poor (but I trust now rich) mother was buried at Hessle. The Lord knows I was her darling son; but, alas! for many years I was no comfort to her. But years before her death Christ washed me from my sins in his most precious blood, and now I entertain a hope of meeting her in heaven.'

the end of a gracious Providence, and that was enough. Now, my father never liked to have this circumstance named, though I have often heard him say, 'That lad saved my life.' Afterwards, my mother never liked him to cross the Humber after dark, unless I was with him; so I often had to accompany him when I would much rather have been at a warm fireside, or asleep in bed. *Witnesses*—JOHN THRUSH, LUKE DIXON.

Second.—WILLIAM EARNSHAW.* (1820.)

There were two brothers, Robert and William, sons of Mr. Earnshaw, of Hessle. They were about my own age, and, like myself, they were very fond of bathing. Their mother used to blame me for taking them into the water so often; but it was less my fault than theirs, for they used to fetch me from school—and I have known them give the schoolmaster a shilling to let me go with them. One day, we went to bathe in the drain, and fearing our parents might see us, we went a long way up the bank and then began to swim; at length I heard some one call out 'William Earnshaw is drowning!' I was then a hundred yards from him, but I hastened to the bank and ran as fast as I could, until I got opposite him, when I again plunged into the drain and swam to my young friend's rescue. His brother was weeping, and said, 'All is over with him,' and I thought so too. I could but just see the hair of his head, when I darted at him and gave him a great push, but he was too far gone to take hold of me, so I shoved him on and on, until his brother could reach him, when we put him on the bank and thought he was dead; but he soon began to breathe, and, after a while, came round. At that time I was in great disgrace with Mrs. Earnshaw, and afraid lest, if we told of William's narrow escape, she would never let us go together again, we vowed to keep the affair a profound secret. Soon after this the two brothers were taken ill, and poor William died, and the doctor said this illness was brought on by their too frequent bathing. They didn't bathe half so often as I did, but it was evident their constitution could not bear the water so well as mine. Mr. Earnshaw was a rich man and very liberal, and, I believe, if he had known the real nature of the case, as I have described it, so far from blaming me, he would have rewarded me for what I did for his son. I kept the promise I made to William for upwards of forty years; but as Mr. and Mrs. Earnshaw and their sons are dead, and as a large circle of my friends are wishful to have a list of the lives I have saved, I think I am not doing wrong in recording William's deliverance in this history of my life.

Third.—ROBERT PINCHBECK.* (1822.)

This case was very similar to the one I have just described. Robert, who was about fifteen years old, was a companion and schoolfellow of mine, and was fond of imitating my exploits in the water. One day he told some boys that he could swim across Hessle Harbour; but, in making the attempt, he nearly lost his life. I was about forty yards ahead of him, when I heard some boys cry 'Bob Pinchbeck is drowning.' He had gone down thrice, and was quite exhausted when I got to him, and he was saved, as it were, by the skin of his teeth. I feared he might seize me, and, therefore, I did not take hold of him, but pushed him before until he reached the long grass on the harbour bank. He could not use his limbs, and I thought he was dead, but he soon revived a little. We took him to my father's house and sent for his mother and a doctor; but when they arrived, he was breathing nicely, and after a few hours, he walked home. His father, though vexed by his son's disaster, said to me, 'You must teach him to swim.' I tried hard to do so, but the water always frightened him, and he never made much out at swimming. A few years after this he died of the typhus fever, and I believe his soul went to heaven. *Witnesses*—JOHN CAMPBELL, FRANCIS PINCHBECK.

Fourth —HENRY IBOTSON.* (1824.)

Henry, myself, and others had been bathing in Hessle Harbour, and I had just left the water and dressed, when a cry was raised, 'Ibotson is drowning.' I sprang to him, when he seized me so tightly and closely, that we had a narrow escape from being drowned together. At length I got myself clear, and took him to the bank, amid the shouts and cheers of a great many spectators. We had great difficulty in walking home, and when we got there we had to be put to bed. Mr. Booth, gardener, of Hessle, and who was the next person I rescued, says: 'You may have forgotten, but I well remember, that a few days previous to your saving my life, you saved the life of H. Ibotson. It had well-nigh cost you your life, as he closed in upon you, and took you to the bottom.' A few days after Henry came and thanked me most sincerely for what I had done, and wished me to teach him to swim. I began at once, and he soon got that he could swim across the drain; but it was a long time before he durst venture to swim across the harbour, in which he had so nearly been drowned. . . . . Now, I would ask, why did not some of these spectators render help in this time of need? Could nothing have been done when they saw us sink together, again and again? Within fifty yards there was a boat, with boat-hooks and staves, and could no use have been made of these, to lessen the peril in which myself and the drowning youth were placed? I am convinced that great numbers of people are drowned through spectators not making a little effort at the time. *Witnesses*—GEORGE TWIDDLE, ROBERT RIPLINGTON.

Fifth.—GEORGE BOOTH. (1825.)

He was bathing in the drain at Hessle, when a large tide was being taken in, and he began to sink fast. I was at a great distance when the alarm was given, but I ran to his assistance, plunged into the water, and soon brought him safe to land. Mr. Booth's gratitude has given me the greatest satisfaction. I had not seen him for many years, and had forgotten the circumstance altogether, until I met him at the funeral of R. Pease, Esq., when he said, 'I'm glad to see you once more, Mr. Ellerthorpe. Don't you remember when you leaped into the drain forty years ago, and saved my life?' And in a note I got from him, dated July 31st, 1867, he says, 'Under the blessing of Divine Providence you were instrumental in saving my life. I was sixteen years of age, and in July, 1825, I was bathing in Hessle drain, when a very large tide was being taken in. I shall ever have cause to thank you, as the instrument in God's hands, of saving me from a watery grave.'— GEORGE BOOTH.

Sixth—ROBERT CLEGG. (1825.)

He was both owner and captain of the keel 'Ann Scarborough,' the vessel from which I lost the brush at Clark's Bit. He went one dark night to Moreton, and as he did not return at the time expected, I felt very uneasy about him, and at last I went on the bank of the Trent, in search of him. When I got near Moreton-bite, I thought I heard a groan; and after a long search I found my captain, drunk, half in the water and half on the bank. The tide was half flood, and was then rapidly rising, and had it risen a foot and a half higher, he must have been drowned, as nothing could have saved him. I struggled with him for three quarters of an hour, and after great exertions, I got him fairly on the bank. We were then a mile and a half from our vessel, and did not get on board until three o'clock next morning. A doctor had to be got, and soon the captain began to recover. But the keel was delayed two days. He was afraid lest his wife should get to know the cause of this delay, and he bound me to keep the affair a profound secret. But he often said, afterwards, 'Jack saved my life.' And I am quite sure I did, as no one came near us, and there was no other chance of his being rescued. I never allowed this case to be put in the list of those whom I have saved, but having given a true statement of the case, I think I shall be pardoned for giving it a permanent record here.

Seventh.—NAME NOT KNOWN.* (1826.)

He was a coachman, but his name I never knew. He was conducting some ladies on board the 'Sir Walter Scott,' when, being drunk, he fell overboard, between the smack and the wharf, Irongate, London. There were but seven feet depth of water, and I had to leap from a height of at least sixteen feet; but I succeeded in preserving him from what seemed certain death. He was covered with mud, but was soon washed, and got on some dry clothes. After I had changed my clothes, and drank a glass of whisky, I returned to the vessel, and the ladies and gentlemen gave me a thousand thanks. The captain's name was Nisbet, and ever afterwards he would have given me almost anything; whenever I met him in London, he used to call the attention of his passengers to me, and tell them what I had done. Many a time has he sent for me on board his vessel, and given me as much drink as I would take, and he used to say to the passengers, 'See! this young man jumped over our ship's rail, when there was not more than seven feet of water, and made a rope fast to a man when there was no other way of his being saved. If I had not seen it I could not have believed that any man could have done it.' He often said, 'Whenever you want a berth come to me and I will give you one.' *Witnesses*—THOMAS MACHA, RICHARD BORAS.

Eighth.—CHARLES HIMSWORTH.* (1828.)

At this time, Himsworth and myself belonged to the brig 'Jubilee,' of Hull. We were bosom friends, and very fond of spreeing about, and spent much of our time when ashore in dancing parties and in ballrooms. Whether at Hull or in London, if we could but find a place where there was plenty of noise and a fiddle going, that was the place for us. We have often spent many days' hard earnings in a few hours, amid such scenes. On this occasion he fell from the bows of the 'Jubilee' while a strong ebb tide was running. I jumped in after him, and we both went under a tier of vessels that were hung at the buoy, Battle Bridge, London. We came to the surface, but were soon carried under another tier of vessels, and had not the mate have come to our assistance we should have gone under a third tier, but he came at the last extremity and saved us. Charles belonged to a very respectable family living at Snaith, where I once called to see his mother, who was a widow. Her son Thomas and I became intimate friends, after I had rescued Charles, and he often said he thought as much of me as he did of his own brother. Alas! the two brothers met with untimely deaths. On the morning of January the 25th, 18—, I saw Thomas put out to sea, and in about half an hour the boat capsized, and he and five other men were drowned. Charles got married, and became master of a vessel, but alas! he and the crew were drowned. *Witnesses—*WILLIAM HOWARTH, JOSEPH JOHNSON.

*Ninth.—*JOHN KENT.* (1828.)

He was a native of Hull, and a shipmate of mine on board the 'Westmoreland.' While in a state of intoxication he jumped overboard into the Diamond Harbour, Quebec, intending to swim to land, but sank at a distance from the vessel A boat, manned with foreigners, was passing at the time, and Captain Knill called to them to pick up Kent. They pulled the boat towards him, but Kent, in trying to lay hold of it, missed his grasp, and the next moment he was under the boat. The captain then called to us on the stage, and said, 'Be sharp with your boat, or *the man will be drowned.*' We did not then know who *the man* was, but, with the quickness of true sailors, we were in the boat in a minute. By this time he had been carried to a great distance from the ship, as the ebb tide was running strong and fast. I was forward in the boat, and on reaching the spot where he was last seen, I plunged under the water, and in a moment I saw the man, and was surprised to find it was my friend, John Kent. I dived to a depth of twenty-five feet, and had him right above me; I soon had hold of him, and though I had to swim against the ebb tide, we were soon at the boat's side, when I said to the men, 'Never mind me, pull him into the boat,' but he had such fast hold of my arm that they had to pull us in together, and even then it was with great difficulty they broke his hold of me. He was so far gone that for a long time we did not know whether he was living or dead. At length he showed signs of life, but recovered slowly, and did not work for several days. After twenty-five years' separation, I met Kent in the streets of Hull, and he remembered, with every mark of gratitude, his wonderful deliverance. My arm was much bruised, and almost as black as a coal. I could not lift it as high as my head, and I said to the captain, 'I am afraid I shall not be able to work to-day,' when he kindly said, 'Never mind the work, surely thou's done enough for one day; take care of thy arm,' and he gave me something with which to rub it. It remained stiff for a long time, and gave me great pain. I hope to be pardoned for adding that, I was a great favourite with Captain Knill, and spent many hours with him ashore when I ought to have been aboard taking in timber. He was a kind man and a good captain, and often, after my drunken sprees, he would call me down to the cabin and there talk to me as a father would talk to his son. And these friendly counsels produced a deep impression upon my mind, and did me far more good than a 'blowing up' would have done. Through respect for him, I used to guard against drink, but alas! I was often overcome. I cherish an undying respect for the memory of my dear Captain Knill. *Witnesses*—CAPTAIN J. KNILL, JOHN HICKSON.

Tenth.—GEORGE WILLIAMS.* (1830.)

He was a sailor on board the ship 'Rankin,' belonging, I think, to Gilmore and Rankin. He fell overboard with a timber chain round his neck, and went under a raft of timber. Some men saw him fall overboard, and called for me. I ran as fast as I could, and had to step from one piece of floating timber to another; however, I soon reached him, and brought him up with the chain round his neck. He was completely exhausted, and it was half an hour before he could walk. This man's captain sent for me to give me some money for rescuing one of his crew; but fearing he might stop the sum out of the man's wages, I refused to go; for I did not want anything for what I had done. He was offended, and when ashore told Captain Knill of my refusal. So to please my captain, I went on board the 'Rankin,' when the captain shook hands with me, and said, 'Captain Knill tells me you won't take any money for saving one of my crew. I think you ought. Had you saved my life I would have given you twenty pounds, and I think you ought to take a sovereign for what you have done. Now take it, and I will make him pay me back.' He then sent for the man, who looked wretched and seemed to think I had gone for money; and when his captain said, 'Now, what are you going to give this man for saving your life,' he replied, 'I have nothing to give him.' I didn't want the poor man's money, nor would I have taken any if he had had his pockets full. I then went forward to the crew, when the captain sent us what sailors call 'a mess pot.' I drank a great deal of rum that night, for I had to sup first with one and then with another, and each drank to my good health, and when I left they gave me a good hearty 'English cheer'—such a cheer as only 'jolly sailors' can give. Captain Knill was pleased that I had been so firm in refusing to take any money from the poor man, and it was enough for me that *he* was pleased. And I can declare, most solemnly, that hitherto I have not received so much as a halfpenny from any of those whom I have saved. I have got many a glass of grog, but never any money. *Witnesses*—CAPTAIN J. KNILL, JOHN HICKSON.

Eleventh.—MARY ANN DAY.* (1833.)

She was a little girl, a native of Ulceby, in Lincolnshire, and fell from the 'Magna Charter' steamer into New Holland harbour. I sprang in after her while the paddle-wheels of the steamer were in motion, and brought her ashore, though at a great risk of losing my own life The noise of the paddle-wheels, the screams of the girl's mother, and the confusion and shouts of the passengers, made this a very exciting scene, but it was very soon over, and the little girl, having got some dry clothes on, her mother brought her to me, and said to her, 'Now what will you give this gentleman for saving your life?' when she held out her little chin and, with a full heart, said, 'A *kiss*.' She gave me a kiss, and O, what a kiss it was. I felt myself well paid for my trouble; indeed, I made the remark at the time, that I was never better satisfied than when that child kissed me. 'It is said that Cicero had two courtiers on whom he wished to bestow favours. To one he gave a golden cup, and to the other a kiss. But the one that got the cup was very dissatisfied. He said, 'In the kiss I see something more than the cup, though that is valuable, but in the kiss there is affection, and it betokens better things.' And I am sure I felt a greater sense of delight, and higher satisfaction at the moment when that grateful child kissed me, than I did when my fellow townsmen, with their wonted generosity, presented me with one hundred and thirty guineas, and other mementoes of my doings; all of which I prize most highly, and which I trust will be preserved as heirlooms in my family, as long as the name of Ellerthorpe shall continue. I have been told that this girl is married and has a large family, and that she is now living between Beverly and Hull. Whether this is true I cannot say, but I know she has never paid me a visit, which I think she might have done, supposing the above statement to be correct. Should this meet her eye, it may refresh her memory, and I assure her she would meet with a hearty welcome from her former deliverer, now living at the Humber Dock-gate, Hull. *Witness*—Captain OSWALD JAMES TONY.

Twelfth—HENRICH JENSON.* (1833.)

He was a foreigner, about forty years of age, and fell into the Humber Dock basin, one dark night, in the month of November. I was walking on the dock side at the time, when I heard a splash in the water, and in less time than it takes to write these few lines, I plunged in after him, and found him in a drowning state; I seized him, and with the assistance of some bystanders, soon had him safe on land. He rapidly recovered and I heard no more of him for years, when a man, a foreigner, called at my house and gave me the man's name and thanked me for saving his life. He said, 'If ever Jenson comes to Hull again, you may rest assured he will call and see you, and give you personal thanks.' I said I should be glad to see him, but that I should not take anything from him for the little service I had done him. This case was fully reported in the local papers at the time, and gave rise to a great deal of talk in the town of Hull, and its vicinity, as many well remember. John Barkworth, Esq., timber merchant, of Hull (who had known me from a boy), in company with some other gentlemen, met me one day, and said, 'Well John, you have saved another man,' and turning to those with him, he said, 'Here is a man that never stops, whatever kind of weather blows, but in he plunges and fetches the drowning person out. Look at his last case! On a dark cold night in November, he hears a splash, and in he goes and saves a man. Gentlemen, the town ought to do something handsome for him.' He gave me half-a-crown, and each of the other gentlemen gave me the same sum. As these gentlemen had plenty of money, and as none of them had any connection with the man I had saved, I accepted their gifts, and felt pleased that my services had been acknowledged in the manner I have described.

Witness—JAMES SMITH.

Thirteenth.—ASHLEY TAYLOR.* (1833.)

He was seventy-five years of age, and fell from the landing place of the Grimsby packet, opposite ——— street, Hull. At that time I belonged to the New Holland steamer, and having lost my tide at four o'clock, p.m., I went down to meet the packet which arrived at seven o'clock at night. Mr. R. Curtis, Mr. Lundie, and myself, were walking near where the boat was expected to land, when we heard a great splash in the water, but could not see anything. We ran to the corner of Pier-street, and there we saw something in the water, but nothing stirred. At length Mr. Lundie said, 'I believe it is a man overboard.' I then looked more closely, and sure enough it was a man. He had on one of those old fashioned great coats, with three or four capes, and which were worn by gentlemen's coachmen and boots, forty years ago; and as the capes were blowing about in all directions, it was with great difficulty I found his head. I had to turn him up and down, to the right and left, topsy-turvey, before I could get his head clear. I took him to the 'Piles,' and held him there, until a young man, who now drives a cab in Hull, came to our assistance with a boat. We took the old man to the Humber dock watch-house, and sent for Dr. Buchan, who used the Royal Humane Society's apparatus, and also gave the old man a steam or vapour bath. I stayed with him in my wet clothes till he spoke, and then I went home and got on some dry raiment. During my absence, they took this old man to Mr. Hudson's lodging house, in Humber-street. The night was cold, and the old man had had a warm bath, and to expose him to the night air under such circumstances was enough to kill him. When I arrived from New Holland, at nine o'clock next morning, a person met me and said, 'The old man is dead.' *Witnesses*—RICHARD CURTIS, RICHARD LUNDIE.

Fourteenth.—RICHARD CHAPMAN.* (1834.)

Unlike the last case, Richard was a fine boy, only seven years old: he was the son of the late Mr. Chapman, pilot, and also brother of Mr. Chapman, painter, of Hull. He fell into the water from the Hull Dock Pier. At the time, I was on the deck of my packet, smoking a pipe, when I heard some one call out, 'A boy overboard.' I sprang from the deck, ran to the spot, plunged into the water, and in a few moments I had the boy safe ashore. I then hastened home, got on some dry clothes, and in less than half an hour I had started with the packet for New Holland. When I returned, Mr. Chapman met me and said, 'John, was it you who saved my boy?' I can't say, but I know I saved somebody's boy, is he yours?' I replied. 'Yes,' said the rejoicing father, 'I'm glad you were there, what am I in your debt?' 'Nothing, Mr. Chapman. I am as pleased as you are, and you are quite welcome to what I have done,' was my reply. He then said, 'Come in here and have something to drink,' when we went to the Minerva Hotel. Mr. Chapman pulled a handful of sovereigns from his purse and said, 'Now do take something for saving my boy,' but I again refused, though I believe to this day he would gladly have given me £10 if I would have taken that sum; but I never did take anything from anyone whom I have rescued, though often urged to do so. I think it was on this occasion that I received £1 from the Hull Royal Humane Society. Mr. Collinson, a gentleman, was on the pier when I saved Master Chapman, and he came and asked me what was my name, to what ship I belonged, where I lived, &c. Soon after, I was called by some gentlemen into the Minerva Hotel, where Dr. Wallis shook me by the hand and said, 'I have often heard of you, and it gives me great pleasure to see your face and hear your voice.' He gave me a note to take to the

Trinity House for £1, which I got, and another which I took to Watson and Harrison's bank, where I got another sovereign. I felt pleased with these acknowledgments of my services, and oftener than once after this I was sent to the same places, and got £1 each time, after I had rescued a human life. The funds of the Trinity House were soon exhausted, and several gentlemen requested me to prepare a list of the persons I had saved from drowning at Hull, New Holland, Barton, and Hessle, and to get it signed by living witnesses. The persons saved by me, for which I had received no public acknowledgment, numbered five, and they gave me £5. Altogether I have received eleven sovereigns from the Hull Humane Society for those I rescued in the Humber, and at Hull. *Witnesses*—WILLIAM COLLINSON, THOMAS SPENCE.

Fifteenth.—ROBERT LEESON.* (1834)

He was a young gentleman returning from a musical festival, at York. He fell into New Holland harbour; some said he was in a state of intoxication. I swam to his assistance and soon saved him. He was very ill, and I believe a doctor was fetched from Barrow. When I returned, next morning, he had gone, but had left me *sixpence* with which to get a glass of rum, which I hastily swallowed. My captain was provoked by (what *he* thought) this man's niggardly gift, and said, 'John, why did you drink it? I would have given you a glass of rum without your being indebted to him.' I am told that this gentleman is often in Hull; if he is, I am sorry he has never had gratitude enough to give me a call. I saved his life and he must know it. I may add that a man who could not swim, jumped overboard to rescue this gentleman, and I had almost as much trouble in saving him as I had in saving Leeson. *Witnesses*—JAMES OSWALD, JAMES SORRY.

Sixteenth.—JOSEPH CRABTREE. (1834.)

At this time I belonged to the 'Magna Charter' steamer, and was watchman for the night. When I went on board I was not quite sober, and I lay down on the forecastle. After a while I thought I heard something fall overboard, when I ran on to the deck, but could not see anything. I listened with bated breath, but not a sound could I hear; at length I shouted, but there was no answer. A plank had been put from the 'Ann Scarborough,' into our 'Taffelrail,' and as this plank had fallen down, I thought it was its fall I had heard and nothing else. I got a boat hook and pulled the plank on board our vessel. But after a few moments I thought I heard something stir, and on taking a light I saw Crabtree, who was engineer of the 'Ann Scarborough,' stuck in the mud, for the vessels were dry. I put down a ladder and went to help him, but he was so fast in the mud that I could do nothing with him. So I ran to Lawson's tap-room and got, I think, Robert Hollowman and two other men, to help to get C out of the mud. He was dead drunk, but we soon got him ashore, gave him some brandy, and he was very little worse. The case was kept a profound secret at the time, and for this reason—Crabtree was afraid that if his master should get to know of the affair, he would lose his situation, and as we all thought the same, we promised not to tell any one of it.

Seventeenth.—WILSON.* (1835.)

This boy fell into the Humber Dock basin, and sank between the 'Calder' steamer and the wall. It was about three o'clock one Sabbath afternoon, and hundreds of people were passing to and fro in search of pleasure. I was one hundred yards from the boy when the alarm was given, but I ran as fast as I could, and when I got to the spot, I found great difficulty in getting near because of the press of the people who were anxious to see the drowning youth. Some one said, 'He went down just here,' and in I went, but I had a task to find him because of the thickness of the water. At last I saw him, and brought him up on one side of the packet, and caught hold of the paddle-wheels, when the people, who crowded the deck, rushed to see us, and gave the packet such a 'lurch over' that we were again dipped overhead in the water. I was never nearer being drowned than at this moment; but 'mercy to my rescue flew,' for the captain, who had been asleep in the cabin, rushed on deck, and seeing our peril, called out, 'You are drowning them,' and got them to stand on the other side of the vessel, which lifted us right out of the water. A man then came into the paddle-wheel and took us both out. I was then completely exhausted and quite insensible. When I came to myself I was in the watch-house of the Humber Dock Company, and a doctor was watching over me and administering suitable medical treatment. I cannot tell how long I was in this state, but I had all my clothes pulled or cut off, and I was dangerously ill for several days. The boy was thought to be worse than I was, and in his case they used the Royal Humane Society's apparatus for restoring animation to drowning persons. He soon recovered, but who he was or where he came from I never knew. I remember the doctor told me his name was Wilson. This was regarded by the public as an act of great skill and bravery, and was much talked of at the time. Mrs. Daniel Sykes sent me, through the medium of the editor of the Rockingham newspaper, £1 10s., and I think one of the clubs subscribed *threepence*. *Witnesses*—ISAAC JOHNSON, S. BROMLEY.

Eighteenth.—SARAH HARLAND.* (1835.)

Mrs. H. was a person of great strength and bulk

of frame, weighing fourteen stones; she fell from the pier into the water. Our packet had just arrived from New Holland, and I was forward making the . . . rope fast, when our engineer called out 'Jack, Jack, there is a woman overboard.' He ran aft as fast as he could, and when he got there, he saw me overboard. He often used to say, 'I don't know how that little fellow got past me, for I ran as fast as I could, and yet when I got there he was overboard.' I seized this woman with a firm grip, and bore her to the pier, amid the applause of crowds of people who witnessed the whole occurrence. Some of them said I swam as fast with this big woman in my arms as I did when I went towards her; this I think was impossible, seeing I was but a little man, and that she was such a big heavy woman. Isaac Whittaker, Esq., who saw me rescue her, gave me half-a-crown to get some grog with. But what pleased me far better was, the gratitude of Mrs. H. She resided, if I remember rightly, in Blanket Row, and on going to see her, next morning, I found her ill in bed. She seemed full of gratitude, and that gave me great pleasure. I have often seen her since, and she always acknowledges me as saving her life. *Witness*—ROBERT TODD.

Nineteenth.—ROBERT BROWN.* (1835.)

He was a sailor, from North Shields, and fell overboard, near the Victoria Hotel, Hull, while on watch. It was the first night of Dacrow's Circus appearing in Hull, and Brown's mates had gone ashore, either to see the performance inside, or to hear the music in the streets. I was watchman that night on board the 'Magna Charter' steamer. A heavy gale was blowing from the north, accompanied with sleet storms. While closing the cabin door for the night, I heard a splash, and running aft, I called out, 'Is anyone overboard?' But there was no answer, for the pier was deserted, the people having thronged to the circus. I could not see anything; but at last I thought I heard a voice, and plunging into the water, I soon found poor Brown; indeed he seized me before I was aware of him, and got upon me in such a way that I could not swim, and, I must confess, I was in a great passion. At length I got one arm at liberty, and made for the shore. I turned round and round a great many times, and, at last, after a desperate struggle, which I shall never forget, we reached the steps at the end of the pier. Brown took hold of the rail, walked up the steps, and seemed as if he didn't care about me; I was quite exhausted, and had to hold by the railings for several minutes before I could recover my breath. I then sat down on one of the steps and felt very ill, and I thought I should have died on the spot. I remember seeing the lights, and hearing the music from the shore, but there was no one near to render me any help. Bye-and-bye I recovered a little and *crept* to the top of the steps, where I found poor Brown, crying most piteously. Two men, Joseph Crabtree and John Young, came from Lawson's tap-room, and I asked them to get some drink for the youth, who was in a distressing state, and I would pay for it. They then took him to Mr. Lawson's, while I tried to make my way home; but scarcely had I started, when a great trouble stared me in the face, it was this: Around the circus were thousands of people, and I thought,—what shall I do? I cannot get through that crowd, and if I once fall, I shall never get up again, and I felt that I had not strength to walk round the other way, and I didn't know what to do. However, I had not gone far when, who should I meet, but Joseph Spyby, our engineer. I said, 'O Joe, do help me home, do; I have been overboard saving a young man, and I can scarcely stand. I feel very bad.' He replied, 'Yes, thou has to be drowned, and the sooner the better. There never was such a fool as thou art. Does thou think anybody but theeself would jump overboard a night like this? No! there is not another such a fool in England!' Now, Joe was a kind-hearted, humane man, and the first to help a poor fellow in distress; but such was the way in which he expressed himself as he helped me along the street that terrible night. He took hold of me and got me through the crowd as well as he could. We went to the Humber Tavern, where I got a glass of brandy, and then Spyby took me home. I got a change of raiment and a little rest, and strange to say, I soon felt well again. For this case I received the Royal Humane Society's silver medal, with their thanks on vellum. The case created considerable excitement in Hull, and the late Mr. Loft (father of our late mayor), offered to become one of twelve persons to allow me £2 per week to walk round the pier and docks, so as to be ready to rescue any who might fall into the water. *Witness*—ROBERT TODD.

Twentieth.—ROBERT TETHER. (1836.)

This young man, who is at present second engineer of the steam-ship, 'Dido,' belonging to Wilson and Sons, Hull, shall describe his own deliverance. He thus writes:—'About thirty years ago, and when I was about ten years of age, I was on board of a vessel whilst being launched from a ship-yard on the Humber bank. By some means or other a check rope belonging to the vessel broke, and dragged me into the water. There was no means of my being saved but by the noble "Hero," who immediately jumped into the water, with all his clothes on, and brought me to the shore, which was done at a great risk of his own life. I remember, also, that there was immense shouting and cheering, and that a band of musicians who had been playing at the 'launch,' when they saw Mr. Ellerthorpe bearing me ashore, began playing, "See the Conquering Hero comes."—ROBERT TETHER, July 24th, 1867.'

Twenty-first and Twenty-second.—
GEORGE EMERSON* AND ANN WISE* (1836.)

Emerson, a porter, was conducting Miss Wise, from the 'Magna Charter,' over a plank, when the plank slipped, and both were precipitated into the water. The wind was blowing very strong, and the river was extremely rough at the time. I had just gone into the cabin to change my clothes, when, hearing such a screaming as I had never before heard, I sprang upon the paddle-box, and saw Emerson, but knew nothing of the woman who had also fallen into the water, and whose mother was uttering the most heart-rending shrieks. I leaped from the paddle-box to save the man, when, to my surprise, I found I had thrown my legs right *across the woman's shoulders!* Of course my *first object* now, was to save *her.* I hastily dragged her to the side of the packet, and having put her hand round a piece of iron, I said to her, 'Now hold fast there, for you are safe' I then went to a distance in search of Emerson, and having made a rope fast round him, I was able to hold him up with ease. But the shouting was as great as ever, and I thought,—surely there is some one else overboard! The fact was, the people could not see the woman holding by the iron, and in my efforts to save the man, they thought I had forgotten her; hence their wild shouts. The engineer came to the vessel's side and shouted, 'There is the woman yet,' when I replied, 'She's all right, come down to the paddle and take hold of her.' He came and took her out, when she had a basket on her arm and a pair of pattens in her hand, just as when she dropped into the water. She suddenly disappeared from the crowd, and I heard no more of her for seven years. Mr. G. Lee. editor of the 'Rockingham, advertised the case in his paper for several weeks, asking the woman, from sheer gratitude, to let him know her name; but there was no response. When I was master of the 'Ann Scarborough,' sailing between Barton and Hessle, I had to fetch (one Sunday afternoon) a gentleman's carriage from Barton to Hessle. We had scarcely started, when a young woman, who was a passenger, said to me, 'You don't know me, Sir, but I know you.' 'And for what do you know me, something good or bad?' 'O good, Sir; don't you remember jumping overboard and saving my life, at Hull? I shall never forget you, and I have come here on purpose to thank you.' I then told her how we had advertised for her name, but could never hear a word of her, when she said, 'My mother and I were strangers in Hull, and as soon as I had got some dry clothes on, we had to start by coach, for Bridlington.' This woman's brother was gardener for Mr. Graborn, solicitor, Barton, and we afterwards became very intimate friends. I have not heard from Ann Wise for many years, but if she is yet living in any part of England, it would gladden my heart to have one more acknowledgment from her. In relating this case at Temperance meetings, I have sometimes created a little mirth, by remarking, 'I went in search of a man, and lo! and behold, I found a woman.' *Witness*—ROBERT TODD.

Twenty-third.—JOHN BAILEY.* (1836.)

He was fourteen years of age, and while playing at the Hull ferry-boat dock, he fell overboard and had a very narrow escape from being drowned. When I first heard the cry, 'A boy overboard,' I was near the Minerva Hotel, and I at once ran to the scene of the disaster. He had been down twice, when I got there, but in a few moments I had hold of him, and brought him ashore, amid the cheers and shouts of hundreds of spectators. I narrowly escaped being drowned. Bailey is now a labouring man in Hull, and I believe the father of a large family. I often meet him, and he always seems glad to see me.

I may here ask, Was it not strange that amongst the hundreds of people who saw this drowning youth, not one was found to render him the least assistance? I do not write boastingly when I say this:—If I could run from the Minerva Hotel to the pier, and save this youth, after he had sank in the water twice, surely those who were near him at the moment when he fell in, might have rendered him some assistance? Indeed some present said, 'We could have swam to him if we had tried.' Then I would ask, 'Why didn't they make a venture?' The conduct of these spectators I regard as being monstrous and unmanly. Englishmen are generally thought to have a fair share of personal courage, but it is nevertheless a fact, that scores of them watched the struggles of this drowning youth, *but took care to watch them only from the shore.* Can we wonder that hundreds are drowned every year along our coasts, if people act as these spectators did. *Witnesses*—JOSEPH CRABTREE, JOHN YOUNG.

Twenty-fourth.—RICHARD LISON.* (1836.)

He was a boy, seven years of age, and fell into the Junction dock, Hull. When the alarm was given, I was at the other side of the present . . . dock, a great distance from where the boy was, but I ran with all speed over the bridge, and when I got to the drowning child, I found he had sunk the third time, and I thought, O, what shall I do? I went in search of him; I dived here, and I dived there, and at length I found him. A cry of joy was raised by the spectators when they saw me fetch him from a great depth, and then carry him towards the shore, on reaching which, some of them received him, and took him to his mother. I heard no more of him until he had grown to manhood; since then he has manifested the warmest gratitude, and treated me with the utmost kindness and respect. For years he was in the employ of the Hull dock company; I had many opportunities of watching his conduct, and always found him a faithful and trusty servant, doing his duty as well in his master's absence as in his presence. This made me think much of him, and I always felt a deep interest in his welfare. He is now in the employ of Martin, Samuelson and Co., Hull. *Witness*—JOHN LUNDIE.

Twenty-fifth.—GEORGE RICKERBY.* (1836.)

He was a youth, and while playing on the east pier, Hull, he fell overbeard. I ran a great distance, and in an almost breathless state leaped from a height of fourteen feet, into seven feet depth of water. I had scarcely touched the water, when he clutched me firmly, and dragged me down, again and again, but I was eager to rescue him, and, thank God, I succeeded. He had fallen upon one of the buoys, and cut his head, which bled profusely, and before I got him ashore I thought he was dead. He continued to bleed for some time, and a doctor was sent for. There was great cheering by the spectators as they saw me bearing through the waters, this bleeding, but still living youth, and some ladies and gentlemen, who had been watching me from the Minerva Hotel, threw out of the window, several shillings and half-crown pieces. . If my memory serves me rightly, I got £1 10s. I thought myself handsomely rewarded; but what pleased me more was the gratitude of the boy's mother; for I have always considered gratitude the richest reward I could receive: more than grateful thanks for what I had done, this poor woman would have found it difficult to have given me, but most grateful she was, and I felt both satisfied and delighted. But let me explain: On going to see the boy, next morning, I found him very ill in bed, and his mother, thinking I had gone for something for saving her child's life, said, 'I have no money to give you, Sir, but my husband's half-pay will be due in a few days, and I'm sure you shall have half of it.' I replied, 'I'm sure I have not come for anything you have, my good woman, for I never take money from those I save, or from their relatives.' She seemed overwhelmed with grateful feelings, and I had some difficulty in persuading her that I did not want money, and that I would not take it if offered me, and I believe, to this day, that if I had said to her, 'You must give me your eight-days' clock and your chest of drawers,' she would willingly have given them to me there and then. *Witness.*—RICHARD CURTIS.

Twenty-Sixth.—MISS HILL. (1836.)

This young woman, when landing at New Holland, ran down the plank, when her foot slipped and she fell into the water, at the low side of the jetty. I sprang to her assistance, but she was fast among some pieces of timber. We were both in great peril, the tide was coming in, and had it reached a foot higher, we should both have been drowned. We were so placed as to be compelled to dive under water before we could reach the shore. I told her that there was no other way of our being saved, and that the attempt must be made at once, and without waiting for her consent, I grasped her in my arm, and under the water we went. The people thought we should have been drowned, but we soon got clear of the jetty; some threw us one thing and some another; at length James Nicholson got into a boat, took us in, and landed us safe ashore. I went to a public-house, where I got a glass of brandy, and borrowed the ostler's clothes, and I ailed nothing afterwards. The young woman remained at New Holland all night, and took her departure next morning, without leaving behind her even a single expression of verbal gratitude for what I had done for her. For some time it was reported that she was the daughter of Sir Rowland Hill, post-master general, but I wrote to that Knight, and found that she did not belong to his family. She made a fine appearance and was well dressed, but when I think of the shabby way in which she left the scene of her distress, I can't call her a lady. I am devoutly grateful that I was the means of saving her, but the case would not have been made thus prominent, had not several gentlemen of Hull, who were present on the occasion, refused to let the case slip. *Witnesses*— ROBERT TODD, Captain THOMAS OSWELL.

Twenty-seventh.—HANNAH WEBSTER.* (1837.)

This I regard as a most wonderful deliverance. Some said she fell, others that she jumped, from the Barton horse-boat into the Ferry-boat dock, Hull. Thomas Spencer, who was working at what was then called 'The knock-em-down jetty,' saw the woman drop into the water, and called out, 'A woman overboard.' I hastened to her and soon got her ashore, when she was completely exhausted, and we sent for a doctor. A gentleman came to me and said 'Did you fetch you woman out of the water?' 'Yes, Sir,' was my reply, when he made this strange and unaccountable remark—'If you had let her stop in I would have given you half-a-crown, but as it is, I shall not give you anything.' 'Thank you, Sir, but I'm glad she's out, notwithstanding; and I would rather save that woman than I would have all the half-crowns in

Hull,' was my indignant reply. I never stood to ask whether a drowning person was rich or poor, friend or foe. drunk or sober. If a person was overboard I did my best to rescue that person from drowning. We took this poor, despised woman to a house in Humber-street, and I gave my word that all expenses should be paid. She lodged in Mill-street, and was a widow, thirty-seven years of age, and had two children. I went to see her next morning, but she had gone, so I had all expenses to pay. I have always thought this woman was one of those poor, unfortunate, and despairing ones, so touchingly described by HOOD:—

> 'Mad from life's history,
> Glad to death's mystery
> Swift to be hurled,
>   Anywhere, anywhere,
> Out of the world.'

Witnesses—WILLIAM TAYLOR, GEORGE HORSEFIELD.

Twenty-eighth.—MISS ELLGARD.° (1837.)

This young woman, who, there is reason to suspect, was a similar character to Mrs. Webster, fell from McDonald's wharf, into Toronto Bay, America. I had in charge at this time a vessel belonging to Mr. Garsiles, and when walking down to the wharf, one cold night, in the month of October, I heard a heavy splash in the water, and the next moment a loud scream. I ran to the place and saw this woman struggling in the water. She was very difficult to get at, but at last I caught hold of her, and soon landed her on the wharf. A man was waiting to receive her, and they instantly walked off. A few days after, however, she called at Mr. Baker's, 'Black Swan' Inn, and asked for me, and on going to the door she told me that I had saved her life, and that she was twenty-nine years of age. Now there had been some strange reports about her and the man who met her; indeed it was commonly believed, in Toronto, that he had pushed her overboard. But she said, 'The report is false. I *fell* overboard.' She thanked me very kindly; I urged her to tell me her name, which she did, after I had promised not to tell anyone; this made me suspect that there was something wrong in connection with her being overboard. She urged me to accept some money. but I would not. for I am sure her gratitude amply satisfied me for what I had done for her. *Witnesses*—THOMAS THOMAS, JOHN BAKER.

Twenty-ninth.—JANE GOUGH.* (1843.)

When seven years old, she fell into Hessle harbour; her mother gave the alarm, and in a few moments I was in the water and saved her. I remember but little about *this case*, but the girl's father often says. when referring to myself, 'That man saved my child's life twice, and the second time was as good as the the first.' I will explain the second case. Miss Gough, many years after her deliverance, married Mr. Shaw, a captain, and together they have brought up a family of children. in respectable circumstances. Mrs. Shaw knew me well, but I had not seen her for many years, when this strange event took place :— I was captain of the Dock Company's steamer, and on going one dark night into the Victoria lock. I found a deep timber laden vessel, with her stem upon the bank and her stern in the channel, and she was rapidly filling with water. I at once went to her assistance. and having fastened a strong rope to her, and then to my packet. I tried, first in one way and then in another, to pull her off, but she seemed immoveable; and I began to fear I should not accomplish my object. But I always believed in that little catch,

'Have you not succeeded yet?
Try, try again.'

and *we did* try again; and after trying many ways but in vain, we put the tow-rope on board, and running our packet at full speed, off the vessel came. All this time there was no person on board except the captain's wife and her children. So I put them ashore, and went on board the vessel myself, and let go the anchor. Now, I did not know who the woman was until she offered me a sum of money, for what I had done. I told her I did not want aught, and that she was heartily welcome to the timely service I had rendered her. She then said—and I shall never forget it—'Mr. Ellerthorpe, you don't seem to know who I am?' I said. 'No, I don't;' when, to my surprise, she answered, 'I am that little girl, Jane Gough, whom you saved from drowning in Hessle harbour.' My feelings were indescribably pleasant and joyous. *Witnesses*—JANE SHAW, JOHN GOUGH.

Thirtieth—WILLIAM TURNER. (1844.)

This deliverance took place one dark night, when we were rounding Flambro Head, and while a strong wind was blowing and a heavy sea rolling. Turner, while doing something at the main sheet, fell over the vessel's side. I caught him, and got him on board, with a quickness that has always surprised me. Mr. Turner, who is at present foreman of the Humber Dock Company, Wharfage department, thus writes:—'I am one of the persons whom Mr. Ellerthorpe has saved from a watery grave. In the year 1844, and during a voyage from Scarborough to Hull, in the yacht, "Gossamer," I fell overboard while crossing Burlington Bay. He sprang to my assistance and saved me, otherwise I should have been drowned. I remember also, when coming over the Humber Dock Bridge, one night, about nine o'clock, I saw an old lady fall from a height of about twenty feet, into the lock-pit. Soon after I heard a tremendous splash, and to my surprise, I found it was "Our Hero," who had plunged his carcase into the lock to rescue the old lady from her perilous position, which he did manfully. I also saw him rescue John Eaby. In the great and terrible struggle which took place in the water, Mr. Ellerthorpe bore up with the greatest coolness imaginable, although at a great risk of losing his life.—WILLIAM TURNER.'

Thirty-first.—JOHN ELLERTHORPE. (1846.)

He was my son, and first-born child. Mr. G. Lee, the gentleman who first gave me employment in connection with the Hull Dock Company, had engaged me to teach his son the art of swimming. We went to the Stone Ferry Baths, for that purpose, and wishful that my own sons should learn this invaluable art, I took John with us. When we got to the baths, I found the water was too warm to bathe in, so Mr. Lee and myself went into one of the adjoining rooms and had a long conversation about swimming, while the two boys were left behind. At length I went to test the temperature of the water, it was remarkably clear, and, to my horror, I saw my son prostrate at the bottom of the bath! My feelings can be better imagined than described. Instantly, and without either throwing off a single garment or putting my watch from my pocket, I plunged into the bath and brought him up. He was full of water, and frothed at the mouth, and was very ill for a long time after. *Witness*—Mr. G. B. LEE, Jun.

Thirty-second.—THOMAS ROBINSON.* (1846.)

He belonged to a schooner, lying in the Junction Dock, Hull. I was walking near the dock, when I saw a great many people running from every direction, and was soon told that a man had fallen overboard. I ran to the spot, and for some time I could not ascertain the nature of the case. At length the captain of the schooner, said, 'He went down close to the vessel, and has been seen twice' Instantly I dived to the bottom of the dock, but could not see him. I swam to and fro for some time, and at last saw him under the vessel; he seemed quite dead, but I seized him and brought him up. They were busy with the grappling irons, but as he was under the vessel, the probability is he would never have been got out of the water alive. I went home and got some dry clothes on, and when I returned and inquired how he was, I was told he rapidly recovered. I have never seen this young man, or heard a word of him from that day to the present. He was a sailor, and may have been in Hull since then, but if he has, he never made himself known to me. *Witnesses*—JOHN MOODY, JOHN KIDD.

Thirty-third.—WATSON.* (1846.)

While going on the Humber bank, to Hessle, I passed some youths who were bathing, but took little or no notice of them until I had got about 300 yards past them, when I saw some men running from a field close by, and heard a youth call out, 'A boy is drowning.' I ran back, and swam to the lad, and soon brought him out and laid him on the bank. I drank a glass of grog and smoked a pipe, and then returned to Hull, for a change of raiment. I caught a severe cold on this occasion, for I had got half way to Hessle when I saved this boy, and had on my wet clothes for nearly three hours. I have never, that I am aware of, seen that boy since. Nor am I quite certain about his name; some one said they called him Watson; but a man who saw me save him told me he would let me know the boy's right name, but he never did. Somebody disputed my saving the lad, so I got a paper signed by a man who witnessed the whole affair, and whose name was Johnson. *Witness* —Mr. JOHNSON.

Thirty-fourth.—SAMUEL DAVIS. (Nov. 6, 1850.)

He was employed on board a 'mud tug' that was used for removing mud from Hull Harbour into the Humber. I saw this tug in a sinking state, and called out to the men to escape from her at once. All left her and got into a boat, except Davis; he was rather lame, but had time enough to make his escape as well as the rest. The men had not left the 'tug' more than five minutes, when she capsized, and Davis was thrown into the water. I was on board a 'tow boat' at the time, and between the drowning man and myself. there lay three heavily-loaded ballast lighters. I turned my steamer astern, and by jumping from one lighter to another, I soon reached Davis. I felt confident I could save him, and having a mud scraper in my hand, I threw the end of it to him, and said, 'Now, don't be afraid, you'll soon be all right.' I did save him, but alas!—and my hand trembles while I write it—the first utterance that fell from his lips was a fearful oath, 'D—— my eyes!' O, how grieved I was to hear a man, just at the point of death, utter such an expressison. We soon got him on board of our packet, and put him in some warm and dry clothes. On Friday night, December the 6th, 1867. a fire broke out in Hull, and my son Joseph was there, and sprung the rattle, giving the alarm, and the first man that came to the spot was Davis. One of my son's companions called out, 'Ellerthorpe!' when Davis said, 'Is John Ellerthorpe that young man's father?' 'Yes,' was the reply. 'Ah!' said Davis, 'he saved my life, and but for him I should not have been here to-night.' I trust the Lord will yet save him, and that I shall meet him and others whom I have rescued, at the right hand of the great Judge.

Thirty-fifth.—A BOY—NAME UNKNOWN.*(1850.)

At this time I was captain of the Hull Dock steam tug. One night, about eleven o'clock, the railway goods station was on fire, and I was summoned from my bed to go and remove our packet, which was moored close to where the fire had broken out. In the space of two hours, three men fell overboard, all of whom I rescued, with the assistance of others. Soon after I had to take the Dock Company's fire-engine on board our packet, as they could not find enough water on shore. The wind was blowing a heavy gale, and before I could get the packet to a convenient place, sufficient water had been found, and the engine was not needed. While I was busy with the packet, a man was drowned, and I felt greatly distressed on his account. So I went and sat down on the paddle-box and placed a boat hook at my side, to be ready should any one fall into the water. I had not sat many moments when I saw a youth, about seventeen years of age, fall overboard. I jumped from the paddle-box on to the dock wall, and ran as fast as I could to the spot. While the fire was blazing before me I could see the boy distinctly, but when I got past the fire it was pitchy dark, and I lost all trace of the drowning youth. Thousands of people were thronging and shouting in every direction, and I lost all hopes of saving the youth, who was now submerged in the water. But when I could not get any further, for the press of the people, I threw in the boat hook; it was eighteen feet long and the tide was very high. I knelt with one knee on the wall, and felt the boy at about fifteen feet under water. The hook caught the bottom of his waistcort, and I felt him take hold of it with both his hands. I never could ascertain the boy's name, but the whole case was fully reported in the local newspapers at the time, and hundreds, yea, thousands of people now in Hull, well remember it. Witnessed by thousands.

Thirty-sixth.—GEORGE PEPPER.* (1852.)

George was the son of my shipmate, who witnessed the whole affair. He was a scholar in the Trinity

House school, but it being Easter Monday, he had a holiday, and came to spend the afternoon on board, with his father. The packet started suddenly, and the rope by which she had been fastened to the pier, struck the boy, and overboard he went. The packet was in motion, but I leaped into the water, while George's father went to fetch a boat hook, but it is my opinion the boy would have been drowned had I waited for the hook. The boy's father was a good swimmer, but he has often told me that he always wanted to think a few moments before he durst leap into the water. However, I saved his son in a few moments, and without much difficulty; indeed, when his mother said to him, 'George, what did you think when you was in the water?' he replied, 'O, mother, I hadn't time to think, for Mr. Ellerthorpe caught me directly.' Next morning, George was ready for school and I was ready for my work, and scarcely any one knew aught of the affair. The fact was, both Pepper and myself were to blame in not warning the boy of the danger that had nearly cost him his life. George is now a young man, and sails, I believe, from the port of Hull, and he seems to think as much of his deliverance now as he did fifteen years ago. *Witness* —HENRY BOLTON.

Thirty-seventh.—ROBERT WOODMAN.* (1854.)

He was a youth belonging to the brig 'Janet,' of South Shields, which was leaving the Victoria Dock, Hull, and he had the misfortune, while unfastening the check-rope, attached to the 'Dolphin,' to fall overboard. For some time he struggled in the water, helpless, and it was apparent that he was drowning. At the time I was on board the Dock Company's tug, which was about thirty yards from the spot, when, fortunately, I happened to see the youth, and I immediately sprang into the water with all my clothes on. I succeeded in seizing the boy as he was sinking, and placed him in such a position as enabled me to keep him above the water, when I made the best of my way to the brig's boat, a few yards off. The poor lad, in his almost insensible state, got upon my head and clung to me tightly, and in a few moments, so entwined himself around my arms as to render me almost incapable of swimming, and the probability at that time was, that both of us would be drowned. I saw and felt my perilous position, as he threatened to draw me again into the water, by his desperate struggles; but at last, with the strength and force of desperation, I managed to reach the painter of the boat, which fortunately being 'taut' from the ring, enabled me to raise myself and the youth out of the water, and we were both got into the boat, though in a most exhausted condition; indeed I had to be conveyed home. The boy soon recovered and left the dock the next tide, and I never saw him again. But I wrote to the captain of the ship, and received this beautiful letter from the youth's father:—

My Dear Sir,—The captain of the brig 'Janet' has sent me the very kind letter from you, wishing to know the age and name of my boy, which I am glad to tell you. His name is Robert Woodman, and he is seventeen years of age. I live in London, and I am very sorry to tell you that it is not in my power to give you anything or I would most gladly have done so. But do accept my sincere thanks; and I do hope, Sir, that if it should please God to spare my son to manhood, that he will in some way present you a proof of his gratitude for the great deed of daring that you have done for him; for the captain said the boy could not have been saved had it not been for you. Please to accept my most grateful thanks for your great kindness to my poor boy. Yours truly, WOODMAN.

Now, I can truthfully say, that this letter paid me well for the great risk I had run, as it gave me great pleasure. Some time after, the 'Janet' returned to Hull, and I went on board to see if I could find the youth, but the bird had flown, for the captain told me he had run away from his ship, and that he had no idea where he was. The captain was glad to see me and wanted me to have a glass of grog, but I refused, having become, a short time before, a pledged abstainer from all intoxicating drinks.

Thirty-eight.—ANN MARTIN.* (1860.)

While the Humber Dock gate was being closed, this woman, who was forty-eight years of age, came up to the bridge, and refusing to wait until the proper time for passing, she attempted to step from one half of the bridge to the other, and in making the attempt, she fell, head first, into the water below. It was high tide at the time, and she was rapidly carried away by the stream. The night was dark and I was very ill, but when I heard that a woman was overboard, I ran to the spot; but alas! I could not see her, and for a moment I thought there was no chance of saving her. But knowing that assistance must be immediately rendered or the woman would be out of sight, and beyond the reach of help, I plunged into the water and soon brought her to the bridge. They let down a boat hook to which we both clung, and then a ladder, up which to ascend. But I told them I would rather have a boat, which was soon brought and we were landed in safety. While clinging to the hook, the woman, as might be expected, was full of alarm, but I knew she was safe enough, so to allay her fears, and wile away a few moments of painful, but unavoidable waiting, I jocosely said to her, 'Hold fast now, Missus. You are as safe now as though you were watching the pot boil over.' She afterwards told me that the most pleasant sensation she ever experienced in her life, was at the moment when she felt some one had hold of her in the water. This woman has manifested the liveliest gratitude for what I did for her, and she never crosses the bridge without calling at my house to enquire after me, and she often says, to my good wife, 'You know I aint right if I don't see the master about.' She was very poor at the time I saved her, but on the following Christmas she brought me a *duck* for my dinner. I refused to take it, for I knew she could not afford to give me it; but she said, 'You must take it; I meant giving you a GOOSE, but I could'nt afford to buy one. Now do take the duck, do, Sir.' I saw it would grieve her if I refused, so I took it; *and this is the first, and only occasion that I have taken aught from those whom I have rescued.* And I am sure in this case, it was more blessed to give than it was to receive, for the woman was both satisfied and delighted. The gratitude of this poor woman, and also that of her family, seems unabated. *Witness*—WILLIAM TURNER.

Thirty-ninth.—JOHN EABY.* (July 30, 1861.)

Police Constable Green, 69, was on duty at the South-end about half-past ten o'clock, on the morning of the above date, and about one hour before high water, when he saw Eaby, in a fit, fall from the quay into the Humber Dock basin. He immediately called out, 'A man overboard,' and with the assistance of another man, got the grapplings and caught hold of Eaby by his clothes, but he being of great weight, they tore asunder, and he again dropped into the water. Green then called for further assistance, when our friend ran to the rescue, and urged by Eaby's fearful condition, and the benevolent feelings of his own noble spirit, he immediately jumped into the water and seized the drowning man. From the effects of the fit, the man struggled desperately. Our friend tried to get a rope round him, but could not; he got his hand into his preserver's mouth, and would have drowned him, had not Mr. Ellerthorpe had so many opportunities of trial in such cases. Eaby's first expression on coming out of his fit was, 'What are you doing here?' when his deliverer replied,

'Havn't I as much right here as you have?' then Eaby went off into another fit. By this time a boatman, named John Tickells, came to our friend's assistance, and was joined by Robert Ash, gateman, Humber Dock, who slipped the grappling rope into the boat. They then both seized Eaby, and got him into the boat and tied his legs, otherwise, so desperate was he, he would have split the boat up. They then assisted our friend into the boat. Eaby struggled so desperately that the men had great difficulty in holding him in the boat. He was taken to his house, 20, Dagger Lane, where he was attended by Mr. Lowther, surgeon, accompanied by policeman Green. He soon escaped, without clothes, and, followed along the street by a crowd of people, ran into No 11, Fish Street, and got into one of Mr. Alcock's beds. He was thirty-seven years of age, and had been subject to fits for years, which were often very violent.
Witnesses—WILLIAM TURNER, WILLIAM STEADMAN.

This rescue—the last of a large number that Mr. Ellerthorpe was the honoured instrument of achieving—was witnessed by hundreds of spectators, who were filled with admiration and wonder. These were seen in their countenances and heard in their shouts of applause, as he struggled with this poor unfortunate man. Not only so, but it led the public to raise a subscription for Mr. Ellerthorpe. Two working men, Mr. William Turner, and Mr. William Steadman, who witnessed the humane and heroic conduct of their fellow townsman, took the initiative, and how hard they worked, and how nobly they accomplished their object, will be seen from our next chapter.

The above list of thirty-nine persons saved by our friend, contains *three little girls, fifteen youths, six women*, and *fourteen men*, in the strength and vigour of their days; and *one old man* burdened by the weight of seventy-five years.

They were saved at the following places: (America,) Quebec, *two;* Toronto, *one;* Barton, *one;* Castleford, *one;* Humber Bank, *one;* Burlington Bay, *one;* London, *two;* New Holland, *three;* Hessle, *five;* Hull, *twenty-two.*

These deliverances took place in the following years: 1820, *two;* 1822, *one;* 1824, *one;* 1825, *two;* 1826, *one;* 1828, *two;* 1830, *one;* 1833, *three;* 1834, *three;* 1835, *three;* 1836, *seven;* 1837, *two:* 1843, *one;* 1844, *one;* 1846, *three;* 1849-50, *two;* 1852, *one;* 1854, *one;* 1860, *one;* 1861, *one.*

But though Eaby was the last person our friend actually rescued, his readiness to imperil his own life, that he might save the lives of others, did not expire on that ever memorable occasion. A clergyman called to see him, and amongst other things, said, 'Now Ellerthorpe, your work is done; God has honoured you above most men, be satisfied; remember the old adage, "the pitcher goes often to the well, but gets broken at last."' Our friend shook his head and said, 'Do you think, Sir, I could see a man overboard and not plunge in after him? No, Sir.' And though upwards of sixty-one years of age, and suffering acutely at times from his oft exposures in the water and cold, he yet thought as deeply and felt as strongly as ever for his drowning fellow creatures; and on two or three occasions his old zeal rose to furnace heat. In proof of this we give the following extracts from the Hull papers:

A SAILOR DROWNED.—On Monday last, an inquest was held at the Parliament-street Police-station by Mr. P. F. Thorney, the borough coroner, on view of the body of Thomas Bates, who had been a seaman on board the screw steamer 'Irwell.' On Saturday evening, about eight o'clock, the deceased fell from the forecastle deck of the above-named vessel into the Humber Dock lock pit. Mr. John Ellerthorpe, the foreman at the gates, immediately jumped in after him; and though both were taken out within five minutes, by the dock gateman, Bates was pronounced to be dead by Mr. Lowther, surgeon, who was summoned to the spot. A verdict of accidental death was returned.—*Hull News, Feb. 14th,* 1863.

Respecting this case our friend says, 'Mr. Bates spoke to me in the water, and said, "I shall soon be all right," and I thought he would too. The water was piercingly cold, and I went and changed my clothes, and when I returned to see how the poor man was, Dr. Lowther had pronounced him dead. I never felt such a sense of distress as I did at that moment; I did my very best to save him; indeed, Mr. Lowther says, "The man died in an apoplectic fit." It was deeply distressing to see the poor widow, when her husband was pronounced dead; she was overcome by the suddenness of the stroke, and Mr. Dale Brown kindly sent her home in a cab. This man, and Ashly Taylor (aged 75 years), are the only instances out of upwards of forty I have rescued, of death taking place in consequence of their being in the water.'

A MAN IN THE HUMBER DOCK.—Yesterday a man, named George Taylor, who is frequently employed in connection with the landing of fish, &c., and who resides in the 'Trippett,' while in a fit fell into the Humber Dock, at the South-west corner, near to where the 'Alster' steam vessel was lying. His fall was seen by some men who were standing near at the time and they at once got some boat-hooks to draw him out. Mr. Ellerthorpe, the foreman of the Humber Dock Bridge, whose humanity and gallantry in saving people from drowning, has won for him the title of the 'Hero of the Humber,' was ready to plunge in after the poor fellow, had he not been readily recovered by the hooks. On being got on shore, he was brought into the Bridge watch-house and properly attended to. Before recovering he had several fits. He was eventually sent home wrapped in blankets.—*Eastern Morning News*, December 13th, 1866.

MAN OVERBOARD.—About two o'clock on Saturday, whilst Mr. John Ellerthorpe was busy at the Mytongate Bridge passing a vessel through, he heard something splashing in the water, which he thought was a dog. He called out to a lighterman, named George Woolass and another man who were on board of the vessel, to bring a boat and get the animal out. A boat was obtained, and the splashing was found to be caused by a man who had fallen overboard. On getting him out it was found he belonged to one of the fly-boats, and had he remained many seconds more in the water he must have been drowned.— *Hull Advertiser*, March 2nd, 1867.

We have seen in several instances, that our friend, after having rescued the drowning, remained with them until all fears of immediate death were totally dissipated. Indeed his kindly ministrations in the watch-house of the Humber Dock Company, have been scarcely less remarkable than his exploits in saving the drowning from the water. In that room is the 'Royal Humane Society's apparatus for the recovery of persons apparently drowned or dead, accompanied with directions for the proper treatment of such cases.' And there our friend stood for hours together, in his wet clothes, during the piercing cold of winter and the oppressive heat of summer, endeavouring to restore suspended animation. He says, 'I always felt very anxious about those I had rescued, and in dangerous cases generally remained with them until they came round. By remaining in my wet clothes on these occasions I have often seriously damaged my health; but I felt so anxious about them that I often forgot altogether my own wet state. Dr. Henry Gibson says I have seriously injured my constitution by these long exposures in wet clothing, and I am afraid he is right, and that it will shorten my days.'

We give one instance of his ministrations in this watch-house:—

About three o'clock on the morning of July the 23rd, 1865, he suddenly awoke out of a profound sleep, and thought he heard a boy call out, 'There is a man overboard.' He sprang from his bed, threw up the window, but not a person could he see, not a sound could he hear, not a ripple on the water could he discern, to indicate danger. He concluded he had been dreaming, but when about to leave the window he saw one of his fellow workmen running with the grappling iron. The old Spanish proverb says, 'that when a man's house is on fire he does not stay to consider if the shoe pinches,' and so absorbed was our friend by the fear that some one was drowning that, without shoes on his feet, and with nothing but his night shirt to cover him, he ran down stairs, leaped over two chains, thrown across the bridge, and in a few moments he was beside the man with the 'grapplings,' who had also heard the cry but could not tell whence or from whom it had come. The surrounding waters lay calm and undisturbed by a single ripple, and there was nothing to indicate that anyone had sunk. At our friend's request, his companion sprang into a boat, and let down the grappling iron, and, strange to say, brought up MR. THOMAS HOGG, of Ulceby, Lincolnshire. They at first pronounced him dead, but after cleansing his mouth and nostrils he was thought to breathe; he was at once taken to the watch-house, where our friend, with fresh anxiety and awakened hope, applied the Royal Humane Society's apparatus, and with complete success. The process was continued till six o'clock, when scores of persons were gathered round the watch-house. The man then said to Mr. Ellerthorpe, 'Come master, it is time you were in your own house; you're not fit to be here amongst all these folks.' It was not till the man thus spoke that our friend was aware of his half-naked state. All did well on this occasion, but Mr. Ellerthorpe's conduct was exceptionally noble.

The last to claim recognition and reward for his own humane and gallant deeds, Mr. Ellerthorpe has ever proved himself the first and foremost in securing them on behalf of others. The following letter, received in answer to an urgent appeal which he made on behalf of an aged and destitute couple, will illustrate what I mean :—

OFFICE OF COMMITTEE OF PRIVY COUNCIL FOR TRADE,
MARINE DEPARTMENT,
Whitehall, 16th January, 1863.

SIR,—I am directed by the Lords of the Committee of Privy Council for Trade, to acknowledge the receipt of your letter of the 30th ult., calling attention to the fact that the late Charles Anderson, who lost his life in endeavouring to save the lives of others from shipwreck, has left a father and mother unprovided for, and to inform you that my Lords have this day forwarded to the Receiver of Wreck, at Hull, an order for the amount of five pounds (£5) to be paid to the parents of the deceased.

I am, Sir,
Your obedient servant,
JAMES BOOTH.

John Ellerthorpe, Esq.,
Humber Dock Gates, Hull.

In December, of the same year, he made a similar appeal to the Board of Trade, on behalf of some Hull seamen, and received the following answer:—

BOARD OF TRADE, WHITEHALL,
4th February, 1864.

SIR,—I am instructed by the Lords of the Committee of the Privy Council for Trade to acknowledge the receipt of your letter of the 16th December last, calling their Lordships' attention to the services rendered on the 4th December, by some fishermen of Hull, to the crew of the schooner 'John Thomas,' of Carnarvon, and I am to inform you in reply, that my Lords have presented the sum of five pounds (£5) to be divided amongst the crew of the 'Washer,' as a mark of their appreciation of their gallant conduct, and ten pounds (£10) to the owners of the smack as compensation for loss of time, &c.

The Receiver of Wreck has received instructions to pay the above-mentioned sums to the parties in question.

I am, Sir,
Your obedient Servant,
J. H. FARRER.

John Ellerthorpe, Esq.,
Humber Dock Gates,
Kingston-upon-Hull.

The following letter explains itself:—

HUMBER LOCK GATE, HULL.
February 17th, 1863.

To the Secretary of the Royal Humane Society.

SIR,—I take the liberty of addressing you in consequence of an accident having occurred, last week, in the Lock Pit of the Humber Dock Gates, of this town. A man fell from a steamer going out of the Dock, whom I followed into the water in the hope of being able to save his life; but although he was not more than a minute and a half in the water, and he spoke to me when I had hold of him, the surgeon pronounced him to be dead when taken to the men's watch-house close by. A similar instance took place about three years ago. I wish to know if, in a case of this kind, a surgeon is justified in pronouncing life to be extinct without having previously used the means for restoring suspended animation. We have the Royal Humane Society's apparatus always close at hand, but rarely used. Having the honour to hold the Society's silver medal, as well as its testimonial on vellum, and also a silver medal from the Board of Trade for saving life from drowning on many occasions, I feel much interest in this subject; and I shall feel much obliged if you will give me instructions how to proceed in the event of a similar case taking place. I believe the Royal Humane Society issue printed instructions how to treat cases of suspended animation. If you will send me some of them I shall feel greatly obliged to you.

I am, Sir, with respect,
Your obedient servant,
JOHN ELLERTHORPE.

Our friend received the following answer :—

ROYAL HUMANE SOCIETY,
Office, No. 4, Trafalgar-square, W C.
February 18*th*, 1868.

Sir,—In reply to your note of the 17th, I beg to say that in the course of ten days or so, I will send some of the instructions issued by this Society for the treatment of those who are apparently dead from drowning, and you can place them in your room. Of course I am unable to give an opinion as to whether the medical man called in, in the case you refer to, was or was not right, as I am not cognizant of the whole state of the case; but I will suggest that, in all future cases which you may have to treat, you will persevere in your attempts at recovery for at *least* half-an-hour before you give up the patient as dead.

Yours faithfully,
LAMBTON J. H. YOUNG,
MR. J. ELLERTHORPE. Secretary.

CHAPTER VIII.

THE HONOURED HERO.

No labour is ever lost that seeks to promote the welfare of men. At the outset there may be difficulties and opposition, but patience and perseverance will in the end bring their reward. And if the warrior rejoices in the number of his victories, the patriot in the extension of his country's liberties, the statesman in the success of his peculiar polity, and the philanthropist in the mitigation of human woes, how much purer and stronger must be the joy of the man who has been the means of saving the lives of his fellow-creatures? Alexander, Emperor of Russia, whose armies had won many a victory on the field of battle, once rescued a man from drowning, and he ever afterwards said that *that* was the happiest day of his life. As no living individual, perhaps, has saved so many lives, on so many separate and distinct occasions, and under equally perilous circumstances, as our friend, so we may infer that his personal joy was proportionately great. He always did his best to save human life, having made that one of the chief objects of his existence, and he reaped a rich recompense. He says, 'I always thought it as much my duty to try and save the drowning, as it was their duty to try and save themselves; and I always felt myself amply recompensed, and highly satisfied, when I got them out of the water and saw they were all right. Physically, I often felt much exhausted by the efforts I had made, and could eat no food, nor could I take rest, for hours after rescuing the drowning. But I was filled with a pleasure I could not describe; sometimes my feelings found vent in tears, and at other times in loud and hearty laughter; and when questioned as to my feelings, I could only say, "I can't tell you how I feel." I had this thought and feeling running through me, throbbing within me, "I have saved a fellow creature from drowning." And that imparted to me a happiness which no amount of money, and no decorations of honour, could have given me; a happiness which no man can conceive, far less describe, unless he has himself snatched a fellow creature from a watery grave.'

Our friend also reaped a rich reward in the gratitude of many whom he had the pleasure of saving. And we have seen that he could receive no higher gratification than this. King Charles, the First, had such an unhappy manner that, even in granting a favour, he often grieved those whom he obliged. And we know that almost as much depends upon the manner of doing a kindness, as upon the act itself. Indeed, in some instances, even a frank and positive refusal will give less pain than an ungracious and grudgingly bestowed favour. Now, we hesitate not to say that, what Mr. Ellerthorpe did, was kindly and generously done. And he always felt that the cheers of the multitude as he bore the rescued to the shore, and the spontaneous thanks of those whom he had saved, surpassed in value any tribute of money which could have been placed in his hands. Wordsworth, referring to the overflowing gratitude which had gone beyond the worth of the trivial favours bestowed, says :

> 'Alas; the gratitude of men
> Hath oftener left me mourning.'

But our friend performed the noblest deeds, and grateful returns were always as pleasant to him as cold water to a thirsty soul. He says, 'I was always well satisfied if they manifested gratitude, but I must confess, that when they never came near me, nor in any way communicated with me, as was the case with some whom I have saved,—for instance, Mr. Leeson and Miss Hill—I was not satisfied. My pleasure at the remembrance of what I did for them is mixed with pain. It may be a weakness of mine, but an ungrateful man is, in my opinion, one of the biggest sinners in the world. I hate ingratitude, and I can affirm, that no rewards I have received from societies and individuals have ever given me half the pleasure that the gratitude of some of those I rescued gave me.'

And can we wonder that he should thus write? Shakespeare says :—

> 'I hate ingratitude more in a man
> Than lying, vainness, babbling, drunkenness,

> Or any taint of vice whose strong corruption
> Inhabits our frail blood.'

Ingratitude for favours conferred is a most unnatural disposition, and is reproved even by the brute creation; for they manifest a strong instinctive feeling of gratitude towards their benefactors. 'The ox knoweth his owner and the ass his master's crib.' Some time ago, a steamer sunk beneath the surging wave, with upwards of two hundred souls on board. The captain, who was as noble a man as ever steered a vessel, sank with the rest of the passengers and crew. Fortunately, however, he came up again, and seizing a plank, he clung to it until rescued by a vessel that happened to be passing. 'Ah,' said he, on telling the story afterwards, 'If my heart's affection ever clung to anything besides my wife, and my mother, and my child, it was to that plank; it saved my life.' And yet, some forgot our friend, whose skilful hand and brave heart bore them through the foaming waters to land.

All did not. 'You shall lodge in my heart, and I will never ask you for rent,' said a grateful Irishman to one who had done him a favour. And our friend found a welcome and a home in the warmest affections of many of those whom he rescued. The blessing of many who were literally ready to perish came upon him. W. Turner, whom our friend saved in Burlington Bay, says, 'What a mercy it is that God has provided such a man as Mr. Ellerthorpe, to render assistance when assistance is required at his hands; for he is ever willing at any moment, and at the first call, to risk his life. I question whether there is such another man in the world. He has a good and kind heart, and in his general conduct displays kind feelings towards all and everybody. I hope he will remain long with us, and that at last we shall meet him in heaven, never to part again.' Robert Tether, speaking of his deliverance, says, 'Some one said to me on the occasion, "My boy, you ought ever to remember that man," and I do remember him and will never forget him. If I had but a shilling in the world, John Ellerthorpe should have half of it, if he needed it. I can say that from the time he delivered me I have always liked to see him, and I never think the place is right if I do not see him there. He shall never want if I can help him. May he live long, and always have plenty.' These, and similar expressions of gratitude, recorded on former pages of this work, were more valuable, in our friend's estimation, than stores of gold.

Though Mr. Ellerthorpe never urged his claims to public recognition, yet we rejoice to state that his humane and gallant deeds were not permitted to pass unnoticed and unrewarded. Persons of high distinction, and of great authority in the social world, spoke to him words of greeting, commendation, and encouragement. Lord Wenlock, having had recounted to him some of the incidents recorded in the last chapter, said, 'How pleasant it is, Ellerthorpe, to have the satisfaction, while living, of having done our fellow creatures good.'

Captain Wilson, whose gallant conduct enabled him, during the American War, to re-capture his ship, 'Emile St. Pierre,' from a greatly superior force, and who received, for his valorous deed, a silver tea and coffee service from 170 merchants of Liverpool, and also 2,000 guineas from the owners of the 'Emile St. Pierre,' paid a visit to Hull, and requested to have an interview with Mr. Ellerthorpe. In company with Captain Hurst, he went to the Humber Dock Gates to see him. They shook each others hand for some time; at length, Captain Wilson said, 'I'm glad to see you. I have often heard of your bravery in saving your fellow men from drowning, and I have sometimes wished I could see you; you are what I call a brave, clever fellow. They say I have done a clever action, but I may never do another. But your life has been crowded with deeds of gallantry. Go on and prosper, my good fellow, and may God bless you; and rest assured if I again come near where you are, I shall come and see you.' It must have been a pleasing sight to have seen these two men, of brave hearts and noble deeds, grasp hands in recognition of each others services.

Towards the close of the year 1835 the following statement appeared in the Hull newspapers :—

'We understand some gentlemen are interesting themselves in favour of Ellerthorpe by representing his repeated exertions in the cause of humanity, and sending the particular cases to the Royal Humane Society. We shall be ready to receive any subscriptions for the purpose of rewarding one so highly deserving recompense from his fellow men. Ellerthorpe is married and has two children.'—*Nov.* 23, 1835.

The appeal to the Royal Humane Society was sent, and Mr. Ellerthorpe received the following response:—

Society's House,
January 21st, 1836.

The Secretary of the Royal Humane Society is directed to inform John Ellerthorpe that at an adjourned general court of the Institution, held on the 18th inst., the Honorary Medallion of the Society was unanimously conferred on him for his courage and humanity in saving the lives of nine persons at different times.

John Ellerthorpe,
    Barrow, near Barton-on-Humber, Lincoln.

The Medallion bears this inscription :—

ROYAL HUMANE SOCIETY'S THANKS ON VELLUM.

The following testimonial, inscribed on vellum, accompanied the medallion :—

Royal Humane Society,

INSTITUTED 1774.

FOR THE RECOVERY OF PERSONS APPARENTLY DROWNED OR (DEAD).

Patron—The KING.   *Patroness*—The QUEEN.

President—
HIS GRACE THE DUKE OF NORTHUMBERLAND, K.G.

At a General Court holden at the Society's House, Chatham-place, Blackfriars, on Monday, the 18th day of January, 1836.

COLONEL CLITHEROW, *Vice President*, in the chair, it was resolved unanimously—

"That the noble courage and humanity displayed by JOHN ELLERTHORPE, a Seaman of the New Holland Steam Packet, on the 19th of November, 1835, in jumping overboard to the relief of a Sailor, named Robert Brown, at Hull, whose life he saved; and the repeated heroism which Ellerthorpe has on former occasions manifested for the preservation of human life, wholly regardless of the risk he himself incurred, and by which he saved eight persons from drowning, has called forth the most lively admiration of this General Court, and justly entitles him to the Honorary Medallion of the Institution which is hereby unanimously awarded him.

NORTHUMBERLAND, *President*.
BESLELEY WESHOPP, *Secretary*.
JAMES CLITHEROW, *Chairman*.

APPEALS ON BEHALF OF MR. ELLERTHORPE.

In the year 1846, a number of merchants and gentlemen sought to secure for our friend the highest rewards the Royal Humane Society could bestow; but to their application they received the following answer:—

ROYAL HUMANE SOCIETY,
OFFICE NO. 8, TRAFALGAR SQUARE,
8th July, 1846.

DEAR SIR,—In reference to your letter of yesterday's date, I beg to inform you that the pecuniary rewards of this Society are limited to London and its environs. But honorary rewards are given for cases which may occur at any distance, upon the particulars being well authenticated by persons who witnessed the exertions of the claimant.

Should John Ellerthorpe have risked his life on the occasion you now allude to, and thereby merit an *Honorary* Testimonial from the Society, I shall be most happy in submitting the particulars to the committee, on their being forwarded agreeably with the enclosed instruction paper.

I remain, dear Sir,
Yours very obediently,
J. CHARLIER, Sec.

H. D. R. Pease, Esq., J.P.
Hesslewood, near Hull.

A second application was made to the Royal Humane Society, in 1852, when the following reply was returned:—

ROYAL HUMANE SOCIETY,
OFFICE NO. 8, TRAFALGAR SQUARE,
28th September, 1852.

DEAR SIR,—In reply to your letter of yesterday's date, I beg to inform you that the cases alluded to in the statement of John Ellerthorpe are all *out of date* for any reward from this Society. Perhaps you are not aware that he has already received the Silver Medal of this Institution for the case in 1835, which was laid before the committee at the proper period, viz., within one month after the occurrence.

I therefore beg to return you the statements, and remain, dear Sir, yours obediently,

J. CHARLIER,
Sec..

Jas. R. Pease, Esq., Hesslewood, Hull.

In the year 1861, and soon after our friend had rescued John Eaby from a watery grave, the people of Hull made an effort to reward their brave and gallant townsman, who had rescued from their own docks and around the pier, not fewer than twenty-three persons. A committee was formed, under the presidentship of Mr. John Symons, a member of the Town Council, and a man of untiring energy and philanthropic disposition. Mr. Symons thus states the origin and success of this movement :—

'HULL, *Sept* 13*th*, 1867,
72, Queen Street.

DEAR SIR,—I must apologise for my seeming neglect in not complying earlier with your request respecting Mr. Ellerthorpe: the fact is, my public duties allow me but little leisure for writing. However, I will try to refresh my memory as to the way in which that kind, humane, undaunted man, received recognition. In July, 1861, the local papers contained an account of a young man named Eaby, who, while in an apoplectic fit, fell into the dock basin; the tide was running down rapidly and the wind was blowing strong. Mr. Ellerthorpe, while on duty at the dock gates, saw the man struggling and beating the water into foam; he immediately plunged from the wall, and after a fearful struggle between the two, the young man being violently affected, both were saved. This act was witnessed by several people, amongst whom were two warm-hearted working men, named Steadman and Turner. The following day they called upon me, with a written list of twenty-nine lives saved by Mr. Ellerthorpe. The account savoured of romance, but then it was signed by living witnesses, who corroborated the truth of the statements made. The men asked me to assist them in getting up some public demonstration in favour of Mr. Ellerthorpe. I told them I would lend my humble aid, but they must obtain some man of mark for their chairman, to take the initiative. They applied to several gentlemen, but in vain, all refused. They pleaded hard that I would act as chairman, and sooner than allow the thing to die away, I consented, although, at the time, entirely unused to address large public audiences. The mayor, W. Hodge, Esq., granted us the use of a large room at the Town Hall, and then we issued large placards calling upon the people to attend and publicly congratulate Mr. Ellerthorpe on his recent narrow escape, and likewise to open a subscription for presenting him with a testimonial. The meeting was a crowded one, but principally composed of working men. I was not in the least disheartened by this; for long before I had got through the list of persons saved by John Ellerthorpe, the large county-court room rang with cheer after cheer pealing forth ever and anon. When, for the first time, was enrolled the long, distinguished list of lives saved from drowning by the hitherto obscure and humble servant of the Humber Dock Company, such heroism and bravery 'touched' the souls of a few present who could afford to subscribe.

The following letter from Dale Brown, Esq., was then read:—

Pilot Office, Hull, *Aug.* 8, 1861.

SIR,—Having made an engagement for Friday evening before I knew of your meeting, I cannot possibly attend.

Had one of our townsmen returned from India or the Crimea, after destroying half as many lives as Mr. Ellerthorpe has been instrumental in saving, he would have been considered a 'hero,' and rewarded accordingly. Surely it is more blessed to save than to destroy. Should the object of the meeting be to raise a fund for acknowledging Mr. Ellerthorpe's gallantry, I shall gladly contribute my mite. I am, Sir, yours obediently,

Mr. John Symons.   DALE BROWN.

I then recounted the interview with Mr. Ellerthorpe before attending the meeting, when I asked him 'what he wished in the matter,' when he made this reply, 'Sir, I feel sufficiently rewarded in my own breast, without receiving any reward excepting the approbation of heaven, and the satisfaction of having won for myself the gratitude of my fellow townsmen.' This was responded to by loud and long cheering. I then called upon Mr. W. Turner to move the first resolution, and Mr. Steadman to second it, because they were the pioneers of the movement. *Just at this crisis of the meeting John Eaby came forward and publicly thanked Ellerthorpe for what he had done,* which called forth the most exciting cheering. Then the late Rev. Charles Rawlings (Wesleyan) rose from amongst the people, and, in a sententious speech delivered with a stentorian voice, asked, 'How much does the meeting feel towards a testimonial,' and offered the first donation as a proof of *his feeling* for Mr. Ellerthorpe. Our fears were then scattered to the wind; the vessel I saw was well launched. Another gentleman, Mr. Henry Taylor, came forward and said, in anticipation of a subscription being made towards a testimonial to Mr. Ellerthorpe, he had already collected a nucleus of £35. A committee was then formed of which I was chosen chairman, Mr. E. Haller, secretary, and Mr. Taylor, treasurer. Three cheers were then given for the success of the 'Testimonial Fund,' and when I rose and christened John Ellerthorpe, 'The Hero of the Humber,' and 'Champion Life Buoy of England,' the people rose *en masse* cheering in the most enthusiastic manner. The next morning found the Humber Dock foreman a household word. I will not weary you with recapitulating the result of our labours. From the Premier of England down to the humblest dock labourer, all vied with each other in subscribing to the homage of this valorous, humane man.

And, sir, I think a moral may be drawn from this,—that no person, however humble he may be in his circumstances, but has it in his power to bless the world. One man can do so by deeds of valour, another by hard and plodding industry, and a third by thought and mental efforts. It has been well said, 'they build up a loftier population making man more manly.' It is evidently our duty to lend a helping hand in the hour of need, either by our wisdom, power, or benevolence. This thought should act as an incentive, more or less powerful, on each person, and make him restless until he becomes satisfied that he is doing something to ameliorate the condition of his fellow men. Men should thus fulfil their mission until called to receive their reward, namely, 'Rest for their souls under the tree of Life.'

I am, dear Sir, yours respectfully,

Mr. H. Woodcock.   JOHN SYMONS.

The following letter, addressed to Mr. Symons, is given as a specimen of the feeling with which the working men of Hull regarded this movement:—

Hull, *Aug. 9th*, 1861.

Mr. CHAIRMAN,—I cannot let the present opportunity pass without thanking the committee for the movement they have taken in this affair. It shows that such acts of humanity may appear to slumber for a time in the breasts of Englishmen until they can bear it no longer, then out it must come; and permit me to add that the moment I heard of the movement to present some token of respect to Mr. Ellerthorpe, it put me in mind of the time when I was a boy about eight years of age: I was sailing a small boat aside of the steps of what is commonly called, Sand South End, in the old harbour, when I overreached myself and fell in. A boy was with me at the time who ran up the steps and shouted out, 'A boy overboard.' A gentleman, who then lived in Humber Street, was sitting in his front room, he immediately ran out, leaped into the water, took hold of me just as I was going down for the third time, and saved my life from a watery grave. I have always reverenced that gentleman ever since. His name is Mr. Bean, and he was for several years an alderman for the borough. What, then, must be the feelings of the thirty-nine who have been saved at the eminent risk and peril of Mr. Ellerthorpe's life? We may help each other in a pecuniary point of view, but very few amongst us have the nerve, power, and ability to leap into the ocean and render assistance to our fellow men. I have therefore great pleasure in subscribing five shillings towards anything you may be disposed to present Mr. Ellerthorpe with.

I am, my dear Sir, your obedient servant,
WM. ALLEN.

Our friend's name had become familiar as a household word in all circles of society, in the town and neighbourhood of Hull, and great numbers lent their influence to this effort to acknowledge the unequalled bravery of their fellow townsman, whom we must, henceforth acknowledge as the 'Hero of the Humber.' The 'Hull Daily Express' contained the following poetic tribute of respect to our 'Hero.'

'Amid all changes evermore unfolded
By mental throe, by accident of time,
Mankind shall venerate the men who moulded
Heroic actions with an aim sublime!
O! ye who shine along life's desert places,
Who've lived for others' good to help and save,
Affection hails ye with profound embraces
And bows before a brother truly brave!
One whose gallant deeds in noble brotherhood,
Nobler far than warrior's valiant strife,
Have found their own reward in others' good
And proved a blessing in preserving life.

And WHO IS HE of whom this land is proud,
Whose name we honour and whose worth is known?
He's one who does his duty in the crowd,
A worker there—and yet he stands alone!
Without pretension, who by deeds endears
His name afar beyond his native strand,
A son of toil—yet one of Nature's peers!
Whose worth's acknowledged in his native land!
His is the praise well won for gallant action
In saving life along our HUMBER SHORE,
And there are many hearths where recollection
Returns to him in blessings evermore!

And he is worthy!—for in his soul implanted
There is a noble usefulness—his choice
For others' good, which bards of old have chanted
To those who, like him, have made hearts rejoice.
O! should these lines be found in after days—
A tribute to his fair and honoured name—

VOTE OF THANKS FROM THE ROYAL HUMANE SOCIETY.

Let such accord to him the meed of praise,
Tell of his bravery and his worth proclaim!
All honour to thee, ELLERTHORPE, and thine,
And as duty calls thee to thy post each morn,
May good attend thee and its graces shine,
And lead thee upward and thy name adorn.'

The following petition, signed by W. Hodge, Esq., Mayor, and upwards of sixty of the leading ministers, merchants, and gentlemen of Hull, was forwarded to the Royal Humane Society:—

To the Honourable the Court of the
Royal Humane Society.

We, the undersigned, members of the municipal corporation, the Trinity House, and the Dock Company at Kingston-upon-Hull, and merchants of that borough, beg most respectfully to submit to the consideration of your honourable court, the services of John Ellerthorpe, now a foreman in the service of the Dock Company of this borough, who, during the course of the last forty years has, by the providence of God and his own intrepidity, rescued from a watery grave no fewer than twenty-eight persons, often at the great risk of his own life, as may be seen from the statement of particulars hereto annexed.

On a former occasion, on the 18th of January, 1836, you were pleased to award to Ellerthorpe a medallion and certificate on a representation being made to the society of his having saved eight persons from drowning while employed as a mariner in the New Holland Ferry.

Considering that the number of persons he has now saved amounts to twenty-eight, we take the liberty of bringing Ellerthorpe's further claims before your notice, believing that you will think with us that his further successful exertions in the cause of humanity, in saving so many persons from drowning, merit some additional mark of your approval.

We are,
Your honourable court's most obedient servants.

In response to this appeal the society awarded to our 'Hero' an especial vote of thanks, of which more *anon*.

The following appeal was made to Lord Palmerston:

Yarmouth and Rotterdam Steam Packet Office,
Kingston-upon-Hull,
30th August, 1861.

My Lord,—The enclosed documents relate to a series of, perhaps, unequalled acts of daring on the part of an inhabitant, a working man, of this borough, in rescuing persons from drowning. He has succeeded, at the repeated risk of his own life, in saving no fewer than twenty-nine persons from a watery grave.

The Court of the Royal Humane Society having, in respect of the twenty-ninth case, and in reply to the enclosed petition, awarded him their 'Thanks on Vellum,' a committee of his fellow townsmen has been organised to ensure for him some more substantial award.

From you lordship's well-known appreciation of heroic benevolence, the committee has ventured to lay his case before you, in the hope that you would deem it worthy of your distinguished patronage.

I have the honour to be, on the part of the committee,
Your Lordship's
Most humble and obedient servant,
EDWARD HALLER,
Hon. Sec. 'Ellerthorpe Testimonial.'

In reply, *His Lordship* forwarded from the *Royal bounty* the handsome donation of £20. The following is the letter announcing this gift:—

13632 TREASURY, WHITEHALL, S.W.,
61 17th *September*, 1861.

SIR,—I am commanded by the Lords Commissioners to Her Majesty's Treasury to acquaint you that, upon the recommendation of Viscount Palmerston, the Paymaster General has been authorised to pay you the sum of £20, as of Her Majesty's Royal bounty.

I am, Sir, your obedient servant,
GEO. W. HAMILTON.

Mr. John Ellerthorpe, Kingston-upon-Hull.

The Board of Trade was next appealed to as follows:

HULL, 8th *August*, 1861.
To the Right Honourable Thomas Milner Gibson, President of the Board of Trade, London.

HONOURABLE SIR.—I beg most humbly to lay before your honourble Board the case of John Ellerthorpe, foreman of the Humber Dock gates at this place, who saved the life of John Eaby under most trying circumstances, and at great risk of his own life.

On the 30th of July last the said John Eaby was seized with a fit and fell into the dock basin, a depth of nearly twenty feet from the top. John Ellerthorpe, hearing his cries for assistance, spontaneously leaped into the water, and after struggling with the man, in that dangerous condition, eventually succeeded in saving his life.

I likewise humbly beg to inform your honourable Board that this is the twenty-ninth person's life the said John Ellerthorpe has been the exclusive means of saving from a watery grave.

If your honourable Board should deem his actions of humanity worthy of your honourable Board's notice, a committee of the working men of this town is in formation to present him with a memorial, and if your honourable Board consider him worthy of any remuneration, I will communicate the same to the chairman of the committee, who will forward any information your honourable Board may require.

I remain your most humble and obedient servant,
THOMAS RAWLINSON.
2, Wellington-street, Hull.

In answer to this appeal, the Board of Trade, through Sir Emmerson Tennant, struck a silver medal to the honour of Mr. Ellerthorpe.

The Sovereign having awarded our 'Hero' with a gift of £20, and the Royal Humane Society and the Board of Trade having decorated him with their marks of honour, it remained for the inhabitants of Hull to show their appreciation of the humane and gallant deeds of their fellow townsman. Such deeds as our 'Hero' *had* performed are not less heroic than feats of valour on the battle-field, and well deserve *public* recognition as well as reward from private associations.

The long-looked-for presentation took place in the Music Hall, Jarratt Street, Hull, on Wednesday evening, November the 6th, 1861. Upwards of four hundred persons sat down to tea, and the local papers state that greater enthusiasm was, perhaps, never witnessed than during this remarkable meeting. The room was gaily decorated with bannarets, and suspended over the chair was a large flag, bearing the following motto:—

'LONG LIVE ELLERTHORPE, THE HERO OF THE HUMBER!'

Grace having been chanted and justice done to the sumptuous tea, the public meeting began. Mr. John Symons occupied the chair, and he was surrounded on the platform by a large number of ministers, gentlemen, merchants, mechanics, and working men.

The CHAIRMAN said :—It was a common custom of persons not novices situated similarly to himself, to preface their remarks by saying that some person of higher local distinction ought to occupy the honourable position as chairman, and that was his request to the committee. But as such a person was not secured, he felt proud of the position he occupied amongst them. He little thought that the movement would have proved so successful when he embarked in it, for with but little effort we have received the free-will offerings of £170. Of course printing, advertising, and other incidental expenses were incurred, and cannot be dispensed with in order to succeed in similar objects. The Royal Humane Society had awarded to Ellerthorpe an especial vote of thanks; the Board of Trade, through Sir Emmerson Tennant, had struck a silver medal in his honour; and last, but not least, the popular PREMIER of England had forwarded from the royal bounty the handsome donation of £20. Thus the movement so humbly began, resembled the 'little spring in the mountain rock,' which became a brook, a torrent, a wide rolling river. By narrating the lives saved by Ellerthorpe's unprecedented bravery, they had struck a chord in the innermost recesses of the heart of the benevolent portion of the people. He was surprised to find that no one had recognised Ellerthorpe's heroism before. During a period of forty years he had saved the lives of upwards of thirty persons. But however tardily it may appear to some, ultimately, eternal justice will assert itself. John Ellerthorpe never required, never expected any public recognition of his services. The only praise sought by him was—

> 'What nothing earthly gives or can destroy,
> The soul's calm sunshine and the heartfelt joy.'

in being the means of saving so many lives from premature death by drowning. Never let it be said the days of chivalry were over in England while we have such a nobleman as a Lord Beauclerc*

---

* This brave nobleman was at Scarborough during one of the most fearful and disastrous storms that ever swept the Yorkshire coast. He had no sleep on the previous night on account of the storm, and on Saturday he said to a friend 'I shall have a sound sleep to-night.' Alas! before he closed his eyes in sleep, and while nobly endeavouring to rescue a number of drowning sailors, a huge wave carried him out to sea, and he perished in the 'mighty waters.'

of Scarborough, and a commoner called Ellerthorpe at Hull. He believed with those who say that the men who dares the 'tempests' wrath,' and the 'billows' madden'd play' on the errand of saving life, to be as great heroes as those who 'seek for bubble reputation at the cannon's mouth.' He would rather be a bearer of thirty blessings than the hero of one hundred fights. No true history of Hull could be written which did not contain the record of Ellerthorpe's name, and the glorious deeds he had performed. Nor could he conclude without expressing the heartfelt hope that the 'Hero of the Humber' might long live to enjoy the splendid gifts about to be presented to him, and when disease shall overtake him in his declining days, may the contents of that purse procure for him the means whereby his pillow of affliction may be smoothed and softened.

The Rev. C. RAWLINGS then expatiated, in a most powerful address, on the life-saving labours of Mr. Ellerthorpe, which was listened to with a rapt attention, and when he resumed his seat it was amidst a tempest of applause.

Mr. TAYLOR, the treasurer, then presented the gold watch and guard, and a beautiful purse containing one hundred guineas. The Watch bears the following inscription :—

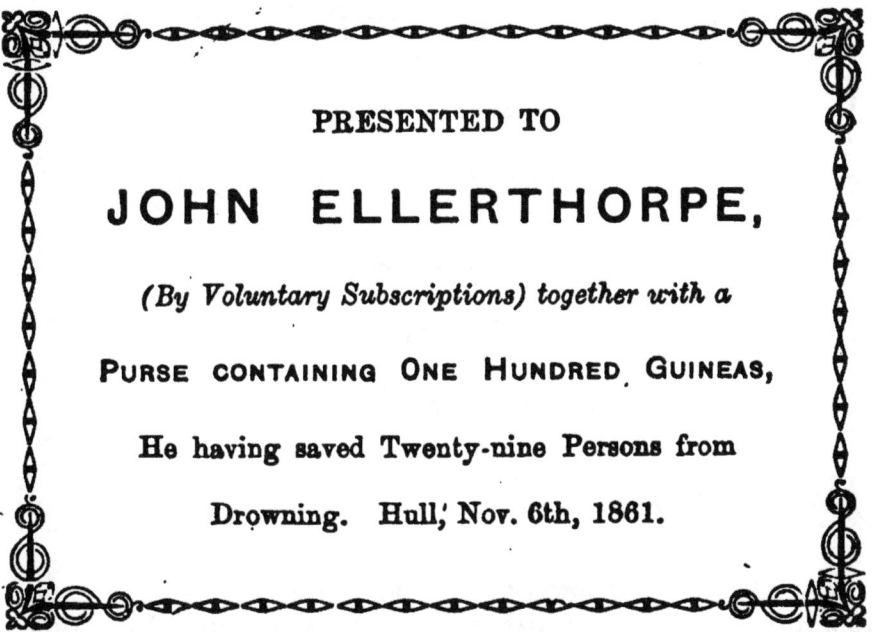

PRESENTED TO

JOHN ELLERTHORPE,

(By Voluntary Subscriptions) together with a

PURSE CONTAINING ONE HUNDRED GUINEAS,

He having saved Twenty-nine Persons from

Drowning. Hull, Nov. 6th, 1861.

THE PURSE BEARS THIS INSCRIPTION :—

THIS PURSE,

CONTAINING

One Hundred Guineas;

ALSO, A

GOLD WATCH & GUARD,

IS PRESENTED TO

JOHN ELLERTHORPE,

Foreman of the Humber Dock Gates,

BY VOLUNTARY SUBSCRIPTIONS,

HE HAVING SAVED

TWENTY-NINE PERSONS FROM BEING DROWNED.

Hull, November 6th, 1861.

Mr. Alderman FOUNTAIN, amid loud applause, and in a few appropriate words, then presented to Mr. Ellerthorpe the following vote of thanks, inscribed on vellum, from the Royal Humane Society :—

Royal Humane Society,

INSTITUTED 1774.

Supported by Voluntary Contributions.

Patron—
HER MAJESTY THE QUEEN.

Vice Patron—
H. R. H. THE DUKE OF CAMBRIDGE, K.G., G.C., M.G.

President—
HIS GRACE THE DUKE OF ARGYLL, K.T.

At a Meeting of the Commmittee of the Royal Humane Society, holden at their Office, 4, Trafalgar Square, on Wednesday, the 21st of August, 1861.

Present—THOS ELD. BAKER, Esq., Treasurer, in the chair. It was resolved unanimously—

"That the noble courage and humanity displayed by JOHN ELLERTHORPE, Foreman of the Humber Dock, in having on the 30th July, 1861, jumped into the Dock Basin at Hull, to the relief of John Eaby, who had accidentally fallen therein, and whose life he saved, has called forth the admiration of this Committee, and justly entitles him to its sincere thanks, inscribed on Vellum, which are hereby awarded, he having already received the Honorary Silver Medallion of this Institution for a similar act in 1835.

ARGYLL, *President.*
LAMBTON J. H. YOUNG, *Secretary.*
THOS. ELD. BAKER, *Chairman.*

The medal, which is said to be a fine specimen of artistic beauty and elegant workmanship, bears the following device :—One side of the medal represents a group on a raft. One of the men is seated on a spar, waving a handkerchief, as a signal to a small boat seen in the distance; another is supporting a sailor who appears in a drowning state. There is also a female holding a child in her arms, the sea having a stormy appearance. The group forms a most interesting allegory. On the obverse side is a large profile of Her Majesty, the border bearing the following inscription :—

'AWARDED BY THE BOARD OF TRADE FOR GALLANTRY IN SAVING LIFE.—V.R.'

Engraved round the edge are the following words :

'PRESENTED TO JOHN ELLERTHORPE IN ACKNOWLEDGMENT OF HIS REPEATED ACTS OF GALLANTRY IN SAVING LIFE. 1861.'

It is enclosed in an elegant Morocco case, the lid of which has inscribed upon it, in gilt letters :—

'BOARD OF TRADE MEDAL FOR GALLANTRY IN SAVING LIFE AT SEA, AWARDED TO JOHN ELLERTHORPE.'

In presenting this handsome testimonial, Mr. Brown said :—

He quite agreed with the Chairman that the last great day alone would reveal the consequences of Ellerthorpe's bravery. He had to present to him what he might fairly call a *national testimonial*, as it was from a branch of our national institutions—the Board of Trade. He had very great pleasure in presenting it to him, and he earnestly prayed that none of his children might ever have to do for him what he had done for his own father. He wished him long life to wear the *medal of honour.*

MR. ELLERTHORPE then advanced to the front of the platform, and with a heart throbbing with hallowed feeling and eyes filled with tears, he said; I cannot find words with which to express adequately the gratitude I feel at so much kindness having been extended to me, not only by the attendance of the large audience I see before me, but by the numerous testimonials that have been presented to me. I never expected any reward for what I have done, and I have before now refused many offers of rewards that have been made to me by the friends of many whom I have been the means, in the hands of God, of rescuing from a watery grave. I do, however, feel proud at receiving these testimonials, and I trust they will be preserved by my children, and by my children's children, as mementos of my country's acknowledgments of the service I have rendered my fellow-creatures; and yet I feel that I derive far more satisfaction from the consciousness that I have done my duty to my fellow-creatures, in their hour of danger, than I do from the splendid presents you have made me. I hope I shall ever be ready in the future to do as I have done in the past, should circumstances require it of me.—He was greeted with loud applause both at the commencement and conclusion of his speech.

A vote of thanks was then passed to the Treasurer and Secretary, Mr. Taylor and Mr. Haller, who responded. The Rev. J. Petty also spoke.

MR. PEARSON (ex-Mayor) then moved a similar vote to the committee. In doing so, he said that it was most remarkable that they had allowed a man like Ellerthorpe to have saved so many as thirty persons from drowning before any public recognition of his services had taken place. As it was, a hundred guineas were far below his merits, and he was sure that the merchants of the town had been remiss in their duty in respect to this matter.

MR. RUFFORD returned thanks on behalf of the committee.

REV. C. RAWLINGS proposed a vote of thanks to the chairman, shaking him warmly by the hand, and congratulating him on the part he had taken in this noble movement.

The CHAIRMAN, in responding, said, he had merely done his duty in the matter; his work had been a pleasure to him, and he had received many valuable lessons, the good impressions of which he hoped would endure in his mind through life. Seeing that we live surrounded with water, and that casualties are occurring almost weekly, he thought it was the duty of the people of Hull to stimulate others to follow Mr. Ellerthorpe's example. He should always look back with pride and pleasure to that evening's meeting.

> 'When time, who steals our years away,
>   Shall steal its pleasures too,
> The memory of the past will stay,
>   And all its joys renew.'

He then called upon the audience to close the present meeting as they did the inaugurating meeting, by cheers for the 'Hero of the Humber and England's Champion Life Buoy,' which was responded to by the company rising, *en masse*, cheering most tumultuously.

The National Anthem was then sung. Mr. Morrison, organist, and a party of vocalists, enlivened the proceedings, which were very liberally interspersed with enthusiastic applause on every mention of the 'Hero's' name.

It is but right to state that the entire sum collected towards the 'Ellerthorpe Testimonial Fund' amounted to £197 10s., and that about £133 in cash was handed over to the 'Hero of the Humber.'

Mr. Hudson, artist, Queen St., presented to Mr. Ellerthorpe a photograph portrait.

CHAPTER IX.

MR. ELLERTHORPE'S GENERAL CHARACTER, DEATH, ETC.

IN physical stature, Mr. Ellerthorpe was about five feet seven inches high, and weighed about ten stones. His build was somewhat slender for a sailor. He stood erect. His countenance was hard and ruddy, and indicated long exposure to weather. His ordinary expression was indicative of kindness, blended with great firmness. When spinning his yarns, or describing his exploits, his eye kindled, and his face, lit up with smiles, was expressive of intense sympathy.

To his wife (who has just followed him to the skies, July, 1880,) he proved himself a kind and provident husband, *i.e. houseband*, as Trench renders the word. Even during his wicked and drunken career he never forgot his matrimonial vow, to 'love, honour, and cherish' the partner of his life; and hence, he never but once took any portion of his regular wages to spend in drink, and the sum he then took was about fifteen shillings.

Of fourteen children, but four survive their parents, two sons and two daughters. The father strove hard to give them what is beyond all price—a good education. His eldest son, (who has long been on the Metropolitan newspaper staff,) when a boy displayed a strong instinctive love of learning, and when, on one occasion, his father urged him to devote less time to his books, and to form the companionship of a a certain youth, he replied, 'No. He spends as much money in cigars as would buy a library, and consumes as much time in smoking them as would enable him to learn half a dozen dead languages.'

Mr. Ellerthorpe proved himself a good servant, discharging his duties faithfully and honourably. During fourteen years he occupied the responsible position of foreman of the Humber Dock Gates, Hull. And when it is borne in mind that Hull is the third port in the kingdom, and that it is annually visited by 30,000 seamen in connection with its foreign and coasting traffic, and that, in the same time, about 20,000 small vessels, connected with the inland navigation, enter and leave the port, it will be seen that the duties of our friend were numerous and important. But the force and transparency of his character, his undoubted honesty, his indefatigable industry, and his unwearied attention to the duties of his office, won for him the confidence and respect of his employers, the esteem of his fellow workers, and the good opinion of the merchants of the port. Dale Brown, Esq., says :—

DOCK OFFICE, HULL,
Sept. 11th, 1867.

Sir,—I have known Mr. John Ellerthorpe as an active, energetic, Christian man, for upwards of eighteen years, and during the past six years he has been under my immediate control.

His wonderful daring and success in saving the lives of drowning persons, have now become matters of history, and have been fully recognised by the late Prime Minister, Lord Palmerston, the Royal Humane Society, and the local officials in Hull, by whom he is best known and valued.

I am, Sir, yours very obediently,
DALE BROWN, Supt. Dock Master.

Rev. Henry Woodcock.

The following appeared in the Hull newspapers, November the 9th, 1864.

'PRESENTATION TO THE 'HERO OF THE HUMBER.'—On the 6th of November, 1861, a public presentation of a gold watch and a purse containing upwards of 100 guineas, was made to Mr. John Ellerthorpe, of Hull, known thenceforth as the 'Hero of the Humber,' on account of his having saved twenty-nine persons from drowning. To commemorate that interesting event, as well as to add another to Mr. Ellerthorpe's well earned honours, a few friends met last Evening at Mr. Rawlinson's, 'Sykes Head,' Wellington Street. After a well-served supper, Mr. Councillor Symons, who, in the absence of Mr. Alderman Fountain, presided, called upon Mr. John Corbitt (of the Air and Calder Company), who presented to Mr. Ellerthorpe a purse containing twenty-three and a half guineas, subscribed by the leading shipping firms of Hull.

'Mr. CORBITT said :—The subscription was proposed by Mr. W. Dyson, sen. (Bannister, Dyson, & Co.), and has been most warmly and heartily taken up by all the leading firms, who were most ready and forward to mark their sense of the obligations of the shipping interest to Mr. Ellerthorpe's assiduous attention to duty, obliging disposition, and untiring activity at his post night and day (Applause). All present knew how valuable those services were, and how much the dispatch of business depended upon them. It had been a pleasing duty to himself to receive the subscriptions, they were tendered in such a willing and hearty spirit (Cheers). Mr. Corbitt then presented to Mr. Ellerthorpe the purse, which contained the following inscription :—

THIS PURSE,

CONTAINING 23½ GUINEAS,

Subscribed by Trading Merchants of Hull,

Was presented by Mr. J. CORBITT to

MR. JOHN ELLERTHORPE,

For his unwearied zeal and attention to the requirements of the Trade of the Port by Penning Vessels in and out of the Humber Dock.

NOV. 8TH, 1864.

Mr. ELLERTHORPE suitably acknowledged the presentation, and thanked Mr. Corbitt and the subscribers for their kindness. As for himself, he had certainly striven to secure the interests of the port, but he had only done his duty, as he hoped he ever should be able to do, without the prospect of any such reward as that. It, however, gave him unfeigned pleasure to find that anything he had done could be so highly appreciated. He hoped to live to advance the interests of the town and of commerce.—Several loyal and complimentary toasts followed, and the proceedings throughout were of a most pleasant and agreeable character."

To the eye of a stranger, our friend's cheerful countenance and erect form, during the last few years of his life, indicated a robust state of health, giving the promise of a green old age. Such, however, was not the case. His employment as Foreman of the Humber Dock Gates, was very arduous, exposing him to all kinds of weather, day and night, according to the tides, and he found it telling seriously upon his health. His frequent plunges into the water, in storm and in calm, at midnight as well as at midday, in times of chilling frost as well as in times of warmth, sometimes top-coated and booted, and at other times undressed, also helped to sap his naturally strong frame.

In a private note he remarked, 'It is with difficulty I can talk, at times, and my breathing is so bad, that I am now unable to address the Band of Hope children. The other night, and after I had been in bed about three hours, I was seized with an attack of shortness of breath which lasted four hours, and I thought I should have died in the struggle. But it pleased the Lord to restore me, and since then I have felt a little better. I now suffer greatly from excitement, and need to be kept still and quiet, but my present situation does not allow me much quiet. In fact, I am afraid, at times, that I shall be forced to leave it, for I think, and so does Dr. Gibson, that the watching, night after night, let the weather be as it may, is too much for me. But I leave myself in the hands of God, knowing that he will never leave me nor forsake me.'

Dr. Gibson, his medical attendant, wrote the writer thus :—

HULL, 26*th* Sept., 1867.

DEAR SIR,—I received your letter this morning, respecting John Ellerthorpe, a man well known for many years past, and greatly esteemed by the people of Hull, on account of his great daring, and humane and gallant conduct in saving such a large number of human lives from drowning.

As his medical attendant, I regret to say, that his frequent plunges into the water, at all seasons of the year, and long exposure in wet clothes, have seriously injured his health and constitution.

After the 'Hero's' death the same gentleman wrote :—' Mr. Ellerthorpe had generously attempted to save the lives of others at the expense of abridging his own life.'

Mr. Ellerthorpe knew the great source of religious strength and salvation, and trusting entirely in the merits of Jesus Christ, he found a satisfying sense of God's saving presence and power to the very last. He would often say, ' my feet are on the Rock of Ages. I cannot sink under such a prop, as bears the world and all things up.' His affliction, water on the chest, and an enlargement of the heart brought on by his frequent plunges into the water, and exposure to wet and cold, was protracted and very severe. He found great difficulty in breathing and had comparatively little rest, day or night, for five months. Dr. Gibson said to him on one occasion, ' Mr. Ellerthorpe, you cannot live long unless I could take out your present heart and give you a new one.' ' Ah,' said he, with the utmost composure, ' that you cannot do.' Often after a night of restlessness and suffering he would say to his dear wife :—' Well, I have lived another night,' to which she would reply, ' O yes, and I hope you will live many more yet.' ' No,' he would say, ' I shall not live many more ; I feel I am going, but it is all right.'

During his last illness he had, as was to be expected, many visitors, but he loved those best who talked most about Jesus. He seemed pained and disappointed when the conversation was about the things of earth, but he was delighted and carried away when it was about the things of heaven. When his medical adviser gave strict orders that visitors should not be allowed to see him, his pale face and lack-lustre eyes grew bright, and he imploringly said, 'Do let those come who can pray and talk about Jesus and heaven.'

The ministers of his own denomination, the Revs. G. Lamb, T. Ratcliffe, T. Newsome, J. Hodgson. F. Rudd and others often visited him, and would have done so much more frequently, but for the nature of his complaint and the orders of his medical attendant. Mr. John Sissons, his first class leader, Mr. Harrison, his devoted companion and fellow labourer in the work of God, and others of his lay brethren, frequently visited him, and all testify to the happy state of soul in which they found him. The Rev. J. Hodgson, in one of his visits, found him in great pain, but breathing out his soul to God in short ejaculatory prayers. His old passion for the conversion of souls was strong in death. Mr. Hodgson told him of some good missionary meetings they had just been holding. 'And how many souls had you saved?' was the ready inquiry. 'You will soon be at home,' said Mr. Harrison, during his last visit, to which he replied, 'Yes, I shall, my lad.' During the Rev. T. Newsome's visit Mr. Ellerthorpe expressed himself as wonderfully happy and anxiously waiting the coming of his Lord. Toplady's well known verse was repeated by the preacher :—

> 'And when I'm to die,
> To Jesus I'll cry;
> For Jesus hath loved me,
> I cannot tell why;
> But this I can find,
> We two are so joined,

He'll not reign in glory
And leave me behind.'

'AH,' said the dying man, now rich in holiness and ready for the skies, 'THAT IS IT.' He soon afterwards expired in the full triumph of faith, on July 15th, 1868.

CHAPTER X.

THE HERO'S FUNERAL.

THE following account of the 'Hero's' funeral is taken, unabridged, from *The Eastern Morning News.*

All that was mortal of John Ellerthorpe, 'The Hero of the Humber,' was on Sunday consigned to the grave. Well did his many noble actions entitle him to the proud and distinguished title by which he was so familiarly known. It may be questioned whether his career has any individual parallel in the world's history. The saviour of forty lives from drowning, during sixty-one years' existence, could not fail to be exalted to the position of a great hero, and the worship which was paid to his heroism assumed no exaggerated form, though it was intense and abiding. He bore his honours meekly, and his funeral partook of the character of the man, unpretending, simple, earnest. No funeral pomp, no feverish excitement, but a solemn, subdued spectacle was witnessed. The highest tribute which could be paid to departed worth was accorded to the memory of the Hero of the Humber. Thousands of his fellow-townsmen followed the funeral *cortege* on its way to the Cemetery, and when the procession reached the last resting-place of the deceased, the number swelled into vast proportions, and a perfect consciousness of the solemnity of the event appeared to influence the conduct of the vast multitude. The silence was deep, and almost unbroken by any sound save the frequent exclamations of sincere regret. No man, however distinguished, has had more solemn homage paid to him than John Ellerthorpe. There were many features of resemblance in the burial of Captain Gravill, and in the Cemetery, not far from each other, now lie the remains of two men whose moral attributes and actions will ever stand conspicuous in the history of men.

The announcement that the *cortege* would leave the residence of the deceased at half-past twelve drew many hundreds to the house, anxious, if possible, to obtain a look at that which contained the body of him whose acquaintance numbers of them had esteemed it an honour to possess. At the time appointed the body was placed in the hearse, and the family and friends of the deceased, as they entered the coaches, were watched by hundreds who sympathised in no common degree with their deep affliction and irreparable loss. The coaches were followed by the gatemen of all the docks and others who had been associated with the deceased. Mr. Dumbell, the Secretary of the Dock Company, Mr. Dale Brown, Superintendent Dock Master, and Mr. Gruby, headed the procession, thus evincing the deep respect they entertained for Mr. Ellerthorpe. Contrary to expectation, the procession proceeded to the Cemetery by the following route:—Railway-street, Kingston-street, Edward's-place, Waverly-street, Thornton-street, Park-street, and Spring-bank. It had been expected that the procession would have gone along the Market-place and Whitefriargate, and thence to the place of interment, and the streets were thronged with an anxious multitude. The disappointment was very great.

When the *cortege* reached Thornton-street, part of the congregation of the Primitive Methodist chapel at which the deceased had been in the habit of worshipping when in health, joined the procession, and at once began to sing. Nothing could exceed the impression of the scene from this point. As the lowly strains arose tears were trickling down many a hard, rough face, whilst a spirit of holy quietude appeared to pervade others. Few funerals have been characterised by greater impressiveness. All the avenues at the cemetery were crowded, and hundreds had been waiting for a long time to meet the procession.

The funeral service was conducted by the Rev. George Lamb, for whom the deceased had long cherished a great affection, and it is needless to say the reverend gentleman was greatly affected. The coffin having been laid in the grave, and the burial service having been read, Mr. Lamb spoke as follows, amidst profound silence :—

'We have come here to-day, my friends, to perform the last duties over the body of the dear friend who has passed away, we doubt not, to a brighter and a better world. The Hero of the Humber, the man who has saved a large number of human beings from a watery grave, who has made many a family rejoice by his heroism, has himself succumbed to the hand of death. But, through the grace of the Lord Jesus Christ he was not afraid to die. I have been frequently comforted as I have conversed with him during his last illness, and have heard him rejoice in the prospect of that hour, and seen his anxiety—yes, his anxiety to leave the present world because he had blooming hope of a brighter and better inheritance. My dear friends, you and I will soon finish our course. The great question we ought to ask ourselves individually is "Am I prepared to die? If my corpse were here, where John Ellerthorpe lies, where would my soul be? Am I prepared for entering the mansions of everlasting bliss?" Many of you know he lived a godless, prayerless and sinful life for many years, but by the gospel of the grace of God his heart became changed. He abandoned his evil ways, consecrated himself at the foot of the cross, to be the Lord's for ever, and by God's saving mercy, he was enabled to hold on his way to the last, rejoicing in the prospect of that hour when he should leave the bed of affliction and this sinful world, to be carried into that clime and those blessed regions where he would be with the saved for ever. That God can change your hearts, my dear friends. Oh, by the side of this open grave, may some here to-day be yielded to God; may you now consecrate yourselves and become the saved of the Lord. God grant his blessing may rest upon the mourning widow and the bereaved family, and that they after the toils of the warfare of earth, may with their dear husband and father be found before the throne of God. May those who have long enjoyed the friendship of our departed brother be ultimately numbered with the blessed in in the kingdom to come.'

Before the mourners departed, the beautifully affecting hymn, beginning with

'Farewell, dear friends, a long farewell,'

was sung.

We may state that most of the ships in the docks indicated respect by hoisting colours half-mast high. —*Eastern Morning News.*

THE END.

WORKS BY THE REV. H. WOODCOCK.

WONDERS OF GRACE;

Or, the Influence of the Holy Spirit manifested in upwards of 350 remarkable conversions. 2/-; 2/6.

'Favourably as Mr. Woodcock is already known by his previous writings, the present work will, we are persuaded, add to his reputation and increase his usefulness. The substance of the work is rich and precious almost beyond praise, and its literary workmanship bears unmistakable evidence of industry, intelligence, and judgment. Its multitudinous facts, drawn from a variety of sources, are skilfully marshalled, are narrated in a lively and agreeable style, and the spirit with which it is animated is deeply religious. It is an exceptionally excellent book, as full of interest as a novel, and yet as religious as a liturgy. People of all ages and conditions will find in its pages a mass of pleasant, instructive, and wholesome reading, fitted in an eminent degree to promote their spiritual growth, and to nourish in their hearts an interest in revivals of evangelical religion.'—Introductory note by the Rev. C. C. M'KECHNIE, Connexional Editor.

'Facts stranger than Fiction stud the pages of this volume, and shed light upon the various ways in which God is pleased to draw men to himself. The work is written in a clear felicitous style, and affords about as agreeable readings as anyone can desire, while its rich illustration and forcible presentation of Gospel truth, cannot fail but prove a blessing. It is in fact, as full of interest as a novel, and yet as religious as a liturgy.'—*Christian Ambassador.*

LONDON: S. W. Partridge, 9, Paternoster Row; Wesleyan Book Room, 66, Paternoster Row; Primitive Methodist Book Room, 6, Sutton Street, Commercial Road, E.; and of all Booksellers.

CPSIA information can be obtained
at www.ICGtesting.com
Printed in the USA
BVHW091030191118
533514BV00008B/940/P